DATE DUE

5/2/2000 IU	
JUL 2 5 2005	

ARCHITECTURE
FOR
WORSHIP

E. A. SOVIK

AUGSBURG PUBLISHING HOUSE
MINNEAPOLIS, MINNESOTA

ARCHITECTURE FOR WORSHIP

Copyight © 1973 Augsburg Publishing House

Library of Congress Catalog Card No. 73-78254

International Standard Book No. 0-8066-1320-3

Manufactured in the United States of America

124994

CONTENTS

PREFACE

After a pause following the building surge of the 1950s and '60s, churches are beginning to plan buildings again. It seems proper to me, and to many others, that they should not simply return to the paths that led to some disillusionment and to the pause itself. This book aims to indicate an alternate path.

The changes of the past decades in the way churches build have been a voyage of discovery, in which the attachment to old patterns has been broken, and a great variety of courses traversed. Now it is possible to discern that the direction of travel has brought us where we didn't expect it to — to a new continent, or the rediscovery of an old one. I have intended to describe the continent here. It is a position different in a rather fundamental way from what have been the customary suppositions of Christians in respect to the places of worship. It proposes that we should no longer build places specifically devoted to the cultic event, or structures which have what is thought of as ecclesiastical character. This is not a personal or revolutionary posture; the course of time and change has brought us to it or, more properly, back to it. But the position has not till now been defined in any book, and this one seeks to do it.

Some of the things I have said and written in the past are now inoperative, in view of what these pages say. And some of the work we and other architects have done is declared to be of less value than we thought at the time it was done. But a good part of what is here said I have said before, as long as twenty years ago, and the past work has led us to where we now are.

I can't cite all the authors who have provided my nourishment in the years since Arnold Flaten generated my interest in the subject at college. I find myself remembering (besides the scriptural record) six scholars: Dix, Davies, Jungmann, Langer, Lietzmann, and Lohmeyer. Another source of ideas is the group of men from three continents whose conversations I have shared. They are theologians, architects, and artists whose wisdom and experience in the arts and in Christian worship are profound and esteemed. The last source is the work I have done with my colleagues over more than two decades in a variety of circumstances for parishes of many Christian denominations. I need to say I am grateful.

Although these pages focus on the architecture for worship, there are implications for the way Christians ought to be thinking about all architecture, and I hope these broader aspects of the book will not be lost.

E. A. Sovik
Northfield, Minnesota

1

The Heritage
of History

If a person is in search of models for present action, he often finds them in past history. This beginning chapter is mostly a study of a period which I think valuable, although it is generally considered a void by the historians of church architecture. Almost nothing was built by the churches of the first three centuries, but they are, nevertheless, very attractive to churchmen, because they start with Jesus, himself, and were centuries of immense vitality. This book proposes to find in these centuries a model for our own; and its thesis is that we ought to stop building cultic buildings in favor of better alternatives.

The Teachings of Jesus

Jesus, as everyone knows, didn't ask his followers to build anything. Indeed on the Mount of Transfiguration he persuaded his disciples not to build some shrines that they thought appropriate.

At another time he talked about tearing the temple

down and rebuilding it, a statement his accusers used as evidence of blasphemy. What he really referred to, when he talked about the temple this way, we are told, was to himself, his person. And this is quite consistent with the other things he said about worship. Worship involves persons, not places. Persons are the temples. They are the holy things. It is in them that the kingdom is present. The encounter with God is any place. And the life in God — the truly religious life — is not a matter of special places, times, or esoteric rituals, but of spirit and truth. And the evidence of this life in God is not the performance of ceremonial sacrifice and the other elaborate ritual observances; the evidence is in teaching, healing, cleansing, feeding, and other good works.

Jesus was a man of prayer; but as we know, his prayer was not limited to the systematic rubrics of cultic religion. He attended synagogue meetings which consisted of reading and of teaching (synagogues were schools rather than shrines). He conducted teaching sessions outside the synagogue as well. He went up to Jerusalem for the great festivals, but the Gospels concentrate on his deeds of teaching and healing rather than his participation in the cultic ritual. In fact the Gospels contain no record of his actual participation in the temple ritual. The story of the cleansing of the temple, often taken to be evidence of Jesus' regard for the ritual formalities associated with the "House of God," and for the particularity of its place, requires a more careful interpretation. The site was the Court of the Gentiles, a place devoted to the people by intention, but then occupied by the tradesmen who were ancillaries to the ritual and ceremonial enterprises. If Jesus was an anti-ritualist, it is no wonder the overflow of ritual adjuncts into the people's court irritated him. And the cleansing act may be understood too, as an eschatological act, preparing for the replacement of the national religion by a universal gospel.

Prayer is one thing, ceremonial routines another. Jesus' concern for people who wished to be in the presence of God is one thing; to suppose that he considered that presence to be focused only in the temple is to ignore the rest of his ministry. All of his life was in the effulgence of God's presence, no matter where he was. And when the gospel account tells of the rending of the Temple veil, the symbolic message is clearly that thenceforth there could be no more a sanctuary; God's presence was not thought of as localized, secret, contained or attached to any particular place.

One question must be answered. If Jesus was *the* anti-ritualist, and if he made the sanctuary as a particular place obsolete, and put an end to the observances of times and seasons, what about the ceremony he himself established, the Eucharist? The church has surrounded it with a framework we call the service or mass and has built elaborate shelters for its celebration.

There is a profound difference between the ceremonies and rites of Old Testament religion and the symbolic event Jesus asked to be his memorial. Jewish religious rites are "esoteric"; that is, their forms fall into a category which is foreign to the remainder of life, and their symbols (whatever their origins may have been) seem arbitrary, useless, or even antisocial. They limit life rather than enlarge it. They use energies and goods in ways which do not serve man. They separate religion and the common life of men.

11

The sacrifice is the epitome of this esoteric kind of ritual. A sacrifice is a strictly "religious" enterprise. It has no counterpart in secular life; it has its own site, called an altar, and its own rituals. Its symbolic power is intense, perhaps because the destruction of life or things, which are its essence, violates ordinary human and humane economy. This symbolic act, and a great many other rituals and ceremonial acts, lead inevitably to the supposition that religion and ordinary life are discontinuous. They lead to an image of God which is radically different from that which was emergent in Jewish history and was taught with revolutionary clarity by Jesus.

The character of Jesus' ritual was quite different. Just as in his parabolic teaching the lessons about God and his kingdom were derived from real or imaginable "secular" models, so the ritual of the church is derived from the ordinary model of the common meal. Its elements are the most commonplace of things, bread and wine, and its original site an upper room in an ordinary structure. Jesus' ritual unites the secular and the holy, implies a continuity between religion and life, proclaims an ubiquitous God, and asserts the possibility that all men may live all their lives in God.

The Early Church

There is evidence in the New Testament that there was disagreement in the very early church about the teachings of Jesus. It was hard for some of the Jews, who had been his followers for three years or less, to commit themselves to so radical a change. But the new covenant prevailed. The posture of freedom from the obligations of ritual laws including the observance of the Sabbath was clearly assumed. The universality of the gospel was asserted — a gospel for Gentiles as well as Jews, for rich and poor, male and female, a faith committed to service instead of sacrifice, unattached to temple or shrine.

The New Testament gives no hint that the Christians of the apostolic age built, or wanted to build, places of worship, or that they designated specific places exclusively for cultic uses. Paul writes, "We are the temple of the living God." Jesus had said that he would be present when two or three gathered in his name. The power of the Holy Spirit accompanied the apostles wherever they moved. The followers of Jesus did not simply represent the presence of God on earth; they were the presence. Any sense of need for a specific locus could scarcely have occurred to them, and the lack of any reference in the New Testament suggests that it didn't. From the beginning they gathered to "break bread" in their homes and other private places. They started to teach and preach in the synagogues, but they soon found themselves excluded. So they met wherever it was convenient. Where they were God was, for his name was Immanuel.

This pattern continued on into the patristic age. And some of the written material still extant declares the position clearly. In a Roman Empire where a great variety of religions existed and a multitude of deities, each with its shrines, temples, altars, and holy places, the Christians saw themselves uniquely as a community of faith *unattached* to any place. Hippolytus wrote about 230 in the *Apostolic Tradition:* "It is not a place that is called 'church,' nor a house made of stones and earth. . . . What then is the church? It is the holy assembly of those who live in righteousness." Clement of Alexandria c. 200 says, "It is not the place but the assembly of the elect that I call the church."

It is customary to assume that the Christians avoided the construction of ecclesiastical buildings in the centuries before Constantine because they were too few to need them (which was not true for very long), or too poor to own them (which was perhaps true in many places for a short while), or too much persecuted. But persecution was not as rigorous or constant as we sometimes imagine. It was not continuous, and it was localized. The first empire-wide action against Christians was in the middle of the third century, and it was much too late to accomplish its aims.

By that time the Mesopotamian state of Osrhoene, whose capital was Edessa, had held Christianity to be the official religion for half a century. And it was in this area, at Dura-Europus, that the earliest known ruins of a Christian church have been discovered. It was a dwelling, converted in 232 to be a small church building.

By the last part of the third century the number of Christians was probably in the millions, and it is known that in many places they had acquired property. Often the home in which a congregation had met was given to them. Some building was done long before Constantine's time also, and though there is evidence of variety in the structures, the evidence seems also to justify a generality or two. One is that the places of worship were domestic in character. One would expect this to be true where the strong tradition of the church was one of worshiping in "borrowed" homes, and where the place was still called *domus ecclesiae,* the house of the church, rather than *domus dei,* the house of God. The other generality scarcely different, is that the places were secular in character; the new buildings were patterned not after the forms of temples or shrines but after the basilicas, which were places of civil assembly.

Indeed, the evidence is that the first buildings of shrine-like or temple-like intentions (we would call them ecclesiastical buildings) built by any Christians were probably the two famous shrines established under Constantine on the Palestinian sites of the Holy Sepulcher and the Nativity.

In 313 the Edict of Milan, Constantine's proclamation of toleration, set the stage for the overwhelming change in churchmanship and in the attitudes toward place, enclosure, and the nature of worship which has given us the tradition of church building that has lasted sixteen hundred years and is just now coming to an end.

The Religion of the Empire

The process of change is understandable enough, however regrettable. Official toleration was followed ten years later by Constantine's baptism and then the establishment of Christianity as the official religion of the Empire. The change that came was a move toward associating God's presence with places rather than with people. The word *church* became the designation not only for a community of people but for the place where they met. The notion of holiness as a quality attached to things and places, which had been held by pagans, was now accepted by Christians. The religious life, which in the earlier times had comprehended all of life, came to be viewed as a separate category, apart from the "secular" life. The cultic event, which in the early church had close affinities to the general communal life of the Christian parishes, began to take on exotic character.

At least three circumstances contributed to the change. In the first place, converts came to the church by multitudes, among them the rich, the powerful, the eminent. Instruction in the faith, which had been a demanding discipline requiring years of demonstrated commitment before baptism, was reduced. If the empire adopted Christianity, the church also adopted and accommodated itself to the empire, compromising in many ways the distinctive qualities of its message and its life. Public dignity and power accrued to the clergy. The institution became not only visible but obvious. The gatherings of the church, which had been private if not clandestine, became public.

Second, the necessity of providing for the assembly of swelling congregations meant that homes and *ad hoc* places were no longer adequate. The practice of building special structures for worship, a practice that had already established roots in the previous century, became the accepted pattern. And when structures are built to shelter a particular enterprise, that enterprise tends to be seen as disparate from other categories of life.

The third factor in the change derived from the immense honor that came to be accorded the memory of martyrs in the period of peace and safety. In the days of persecution martyrdom was considered the ultimate privilege. Now the honor was given architectural and monumental form. The sites of martyrs' deaths or graves gathered an aura of holiness and became favorite places for church buildings. Relics of the martyrs and saints and other "holy" objects were collected; and by the sixth century it was accepted that church buildings were repositories of such things. Inevitably people attributed sanctity to the buildings.

So the division between "sacred" space and "profane" space emerged, reflecting a growing division between religious life and secular life. The study of this revolutionary process is, I think, not complete; and the general understanding does not recognize that the change in the church was catastrophic.

That it came rather hesitantly, and that it took many generations is clear, however. The ambivalence in the writings of church fathers is one evidence. (The works of St. Jerome, for example, contain contradictory views on the subject of shrines.) An interesting letter of Pope Celestine I in 428, saying that a clergyman should not wear special identifying garb in everyday circumstances but should be recognizable by his way of life, suggests that the continuity of sacred and secular was still an ideal. The development of the gorgeous religious images which distinguish early Christian church interiors was not an immediate accomplishment; the famous mosaics at Ravenna, for instance, are sixth century. That interiors were decorated earlier with paintings and mosaics is true, but these were a secular heritage characteristic of domestic architecture, and the Byzantine glory is a new kind of artistic vision. The time when the exteriors of church buildings took forms and acquired details of specifically ecclesiastical character came even later.

The emergence of the monastic movement is recognized as evidence of the sense among thoroughly committed Christians of the time, that the church was no longer the church of the apostles and the fathers of Ante-Nicean centuries, but had become something else.

The church had changed, and as it accommodated itself to the secular establishment, it also accommodated itself to patterns of worship and patterns of architecture which not only obscure the position Jesus and his earlier followers took, but oppose it. The conception of people as the Temple of God was replaced by the notion of holy places. The house of the church became the house of God. The idea of holy things eclipsed the idea of holy people and holy acts. The continuity between secular and sacred was replaced by a strong dichotomy. The sense of life in the eschaton, that paradoxical convergence of present and future in which the early Christians had lived, gave way to a single focus on the kingdom of the next world.

The Reformation

The history of the church building through the Middle Ages is a record of a more explicit expression of a theology, a liturgy, and a piety that contradicted in important ways the essential message of Jesus. And when the Protestant and Catholic reformations of the sixteenth century came, the architectural forms that resulted were only partially corrective. The conservative reformers were at their most conservative in matters of the environment of worship. The destruction of images and relics and the rearrangement of furniture in the existing buildings, and the sharp contrasts of form that appeared in some of the few new places of worship that were built in those times, did not effectively bring the minds of churchmen back into harmony with the mind of the early church.

The lesson to be learned here is that architecture is a more influential factor in the life of society than most people suppose. The incompleteness of the Reformation in terms of architecture was no doubt the result of the longevity of architecture. Buildings stand, and are not easily removed or changed. The "houses of God" from medieval times continued to stand, continued to assert themselves as "houses of God" because of their strong ecclesiastical character, and continued to teach the people around them that there ought to be such a place as a "house of God." Despite what people read or heard of the words of Jesus or the apostles or the Early Fathers, the silent voice of architecture spoke more persuasively.

As far as the environment of worship is concerned, the last four centuries have been the children of the Middle Ages, not the Reformation. And most of the churches have continued to establish "holy places," more or less on the medieval patterns.

Yet the light of the Scripture on the subject has not been fully obscured through these sixteen centuries. There has been some continuous glow, and some sparkling flashes deserve our attention. It is true that down through the centuries church buildings have not been consistently seen as exclusively places of worship. Church buildings have been multi-purpose buildings, houses for the people, used for a variety of public and secular events and activities that nourish the human and "secular" life. They have been used for fairs and festivals, as hospitals and hospices, for civic meetings and secular celebrations. And the people

The late 17th-century Puritan meeting house was secular in form and detail.

have often insisted that the cathedrals and churches were theirs, and not the exclusive domain of the clerics, the ecclesiastical establishment, and the cultic event. The multi-purpose use of churches signifies that Christians have retained the sense that if the Sabbath was made for man, and not man for the Sabbath, so the cultic place should be for man.

From time to time religious groups have explicitly rejected the establishment position and reasserted the New Testament posture. Some of the radical reformers opposed the concept of a particular place of worship and brought their worship back to the homes. The first Mennonite meeting houses in Pennsylvania came long after the settlers had established themselves. They were finally built because none of the farmsteads could provide shelter for all the horses in the cold winters through the three-hour services; and so extensive stables were built with the meeting houses adjacent. The Puritans built meeting houses, quite secular in form and detail, and used them for any public assembly. The early Methodists had their places of worship in any convenient barn or loft, and when they built, their architecture was consciously non-ecclesiastical. In Scotland the custom of locking the church except during services prevailed. When the people were not there, the building was not to be thought of as a place of Divine presence. The church moved with the people to their homes. And everywhere, in innumerable circumstances, Christians have met in *ad hoc* shelters, knowing that the presence of God was not really associated with particular places or places with a particular architectural character.

This is so commonly acknowledged as to be axiomatic. Yet over sixteen centuries most Christians have thought that if possible they should provide a "holy place," a "house of God." It is now time, because we are again in a time of lively renewal of the church, and because we have in the course of a half-century been moving steadily in the direction of recovering the pre-Constantinian position, to redefine the conception of how Christians shelter their liturgies. How we have come in the last decades to a place where this can be done is the subject of the next chapter.

2

The Return
to the Non-Church

About 1840 a curious but very dynamic movement called the Ecclesiological Movement rose in England under the leadership of John Mason Neale, the hymnologist, and some other lively and articulate men. The movement started in England and had a great deal of influence there and on the continent, and in any number of remote corners of the world where Englishmen had their colonial posts, but its influence was most thorough in America. Most of the churches in this country have been built since 1840, and the forms of church building that most Americans have considered "traditional" are the forms which were enthusiastically and effectively promoted by the Ecclesiological Movement.

Pugin, an English architect and a Roman Catholic, had preceded the Ecclesiologists in saying that the Gothic structures of the Middle Ages were the only really appropriate patterns for what was called Christian architecture. Neale and his friends concurred. Gothic

23

architecture was the product, they asserted, of a society whose culture was as nearly Christian as a society could be, undiluted by the pagan attitudes of classical culture as earlier years of the Roman Empire and the later years of Renaissance had been. They called for a return to medieval forms, and set about establishing what they meant by studying, measuring, reconstructing, and publicizing, through drawings and details, the medieval church buildings standing in England. They admitted to the necessity of some change, since they were primarily concerned with buildings for Protestants. But the goals they set were clearly, even dogmatically, prescribed and eagerly accepted.

Their own energies wore thin in little more than a decade. But their literature, the buildings whose design they were able to control, and their enthusiasm carried their ideas far abroad. Their principles were adapted, extended, and amplified by others so that a hundred years later strong echoes of the movement appeared in literature, and the reverberations in architectural form continue to the present.

The characteristic buildings of this neo-gothic adventure are built of stone, with buttresses, high arched vaults of stone or wood and steep roofs, towers, pointed windows with stained glass, an axial plan with a central aisle, a very deep chancel sharply divided from the nave containing a divided choir. There is a good deal of ornamental carving and painting, particularly about the altar which is at the remotest position in the chancel. Thousands of such churches stand in the United States. And in thousands more, selected elements of the Ecclesiological conception are merged with variant plans, structures, or denominational particularities. The word "churchly" is associated in most of our minds with this kind of building.

But other traditions ran parallel and were sometimes preferred. In this country the colonial was the most popular of these, but revivals of other historical styles and eclectic combinations of styles appeared too. All this architecture had something in common. It was derivative in form, and backward rather than forward looking.

Against this conventional ecclesiastical background new things began to happen in this century, and although by now the architecture of churches is so varied that it often seems capricious, I believe that there has been some progress, or at least a directional movement. In the work of the last half century I find a pattern which, if not chronologically systematic, is still subject to analysis. If we reflect on the course through which design has passed, we can discern where we are moving, and ought to move.

Technical and Esthetic Factors

We have been living in an age of technology, and since technical matters are a part of the architect's profession, it isn't surprising that the elements of building that first gave way to the pressures of the new age were technical factors. In the late nineteenth and early twentieth centuries, steel and concrete construction began to replace masonry and timber. The device of concealing steel or concrete skeletons in masonry or wood sheathing then became general. This gave the illusion of ancient forms, but the result is more like stage scenery than authentic architecture. Indeed it is two steps away from authentic architecture: derivative forms built by artificial means.

Notre Dame du le Raincy

Architects who preferred authenticity looked for ways to recover it. In 1908 Frank Lloyd Wright had built Unity Temple in Oak Park, Illinois. It is a forthright concrete structure, but it had little influence among the churches. In 1922 August Perret made drawings for a church in Le Raincy, near Paris, which was to be concrete — partly cast-in-place, and partly precast. He won the competition for the project with a cost estimate far below that of other more conventional designs and saw the church built. It has been considered an early classic, and it inspired other builders to break traditional patterns. But it is really a type of concrete gothic, a medieval conception interpreted in 20th century technology.

Later in the same decade Otto Bartning, a German, was commissioned to design a church for an exposition in Cologne. He used exposed steel framing and a copper panel "curtain wall." It is apparent in this work, too, that the principal achievement was a technical one. Great areas of stained glass were framed in steel rather than in stone tracery. Prefabricated materials allowed construction in four months.

Architectural esthetics have always been to a high degree a response to structure and other technical matters, so it has been inevitable that as a new technology appears, a new esthetic should also. Just as there were early churches of visionary technology, there were examples of visionary esthetic understanding. One noteworthy example was St. Engelbert's Church (1930) in a suburb of Cologne. Here the structure is a series of radiating concrete vaults, elliptical in form rather than pointed or round-headed, sheathed in copper. The building still seems esthetically new; but the plan is basically that of Charlemagne's chapel at Aachen, fifty miles away and 1100 years earlier.

A number of gifted architects have designed famous church buildings with the same virtues and the same limitations through the last forty years. Eliel Saarinen's Christ Lutheran in Minneapolis (1949), Tange's St. Mary's Cathedral in Tokyo (1964), Mies van der Rohe's little chapel in Chicago, and many others are examples of technical and esthetic sophistication coupled with theological and liturgical naivete.

Their newness has been architectonic, the matters that are presumed to be within the province of professional architects. But they have limitations, for this group of buildings does not reflect faithfully the changing understanding of theological perceptions and emphases, ways of worship, and general piety. At its best, architecture should do this also, since at its best the archi-

(Above) St. Engelbert's of Cologne.
(Below) Otto Bartning's Stahlkirche.

tecture of faith has been a consistent image of faith and expresses in space and substance the same attitudes and concepts that the church confesses in words and cult.

It would be wrong not to observe, however, that these transformations of tradition into modern dress, have been in this respect, at least, expressive. They have by their very modernity signified that the church wishes to be understood as a lively institution, related to the currents of life around her, responsive to the twentieth century, speaking the language of the twentieth century. This is a sharp change from the ideals of the Ecclesiological Movement, and the use of secular technology provides in some degree the proper symbol of this posture.

Changing View of the Church

What this kind of change amounts to is a change of grammar and rhetoric, and even if we applaud it, we need to recognize that an architecture which is a faithful image of the church of the twentieth century requires changes more substantial. It needs to reflect the changes in the substance of what the church is thinking and feeling and saying to itself and to the world around it. It is these changes in substance which are bringing the church to a new posture, or more properly, back to a forgotten one.

Otto Bartning, who designed the steel and copper building for the Cologne exhibition, had proposed earlier that the long and narrow processional or axial plans of traditional buildings are inappropriate to Christian understanding. The proper view of the gathered congregation, he said, is that of a cohesive com-

29

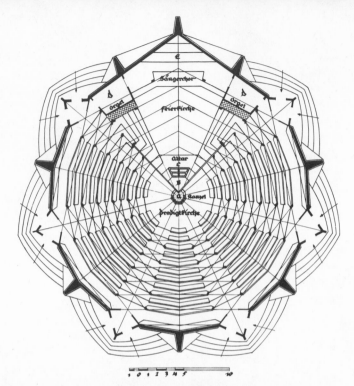

Plan and model for Bartning's Sternkirche

munity of clergy and laymen (all priests) whose members should be aware of their unity as the Body of Christ, the family of God, the household of believers. When they meet it is not as individuals at prayer, and not as a congregation of observers in attendance at a clerical ritual, but as a community acting together. Such a statement has a Pauline resonance; Bartning saw the circular room as the proper reflection of this understanding, for such an architectural shape not only symbolizes unity and coherence, but affectively encourages it. He made a model which he called the *Stern Kirche* with altar at the center and a full ring of people about it. By now this image has been built many times, and its general propriety as a formal expression is broadly accepted.

Its essence is that it is a single unified space, and though it may be articulated into zones or functional areas related to the various liturgical functions — a place for the choir, a place for the eucharist, a place for baptism and so on — it is no longer comprised of nave and chancel. And we would do well to drop the use of those words from all but our historical vocabulary. Such a concept is consistent not only with the words of Scripture, but with the practice of the early church.

The redefinition of the worshiping community in the image of the gathered family has had a parallel in the redefinition of the Eucharist, which relates it to the domestic meal. The Lord's Supper had in the course of history among most Christians acquired a consequentially different character. One way or another it had accrued to itself patterns and implications which made it sometimes a kind of exotic ritual in which domestic associations were lost, and sometimes a kind of personal, private, and penitential experience from which the sense of the celebration of a common life was absent.

Yet its origins were domestic in character, whether in the Passover meal or the common meal, and the very terms we use — *communion* and *celebration* — tell us that it is not essentially a private kind of action.

The reflections on sacramental theology have brought us back to liturgical patterns which are nearer to those of the early church. The "basilican posture," with celebrant facing the congregation across a free-standing table, has never been entirely supplanted, even among the so-called liturgical churches, by the high altar against a remote reredos. It is called the "basilican posture" because it has been in constant use in some of the early Italian basilicas. Now it is generally accepted as the appropriate pattern for several good reasons. The Lord's Table, which is the table of the community, is brought out where it is accessible, and appropriately near, to the community. More and more the practice of kneeling, which as a bodily posture can scarcely be associated either with any sort of domestic meal or with the interpersonal awareness appropriate to a common experience, is being abandoned. Again we are coming back not only to the understanding but toward the liturgical patterns of the early church and the physical arrangements to accommodate them.

The studies in sacramental thought and practice have underlined another view which has its influence on building forms. Sacrament is defined as act rather than thing. A generation ago, when a competition was held for the design of a new cathedral to replace the ancient one at Coventry, which had been destroyed

People are more important than furniture in this Finnish chapel.

in the war, the program described a church structure as essentially "a shelter for an altar." Such a statement was not broadly challenged then; but would be unacceptable now. A house of worship is not a shelter for an altar; it is a shelter for people. It is not the table that makes a sacrament; it is the people and what they do. The things are adjuncts, conveniences, symbols, utensils. The presence of God is not assured by things or by symbols or by buildings, but by Christian people.

If this is so, and if we recognize the relative unimportance of things, and the prime importance of people, and consciously try to keep this order of importance clear, the early Christian use of borrowed spaces and portable equipment and the attempt to achieve domestic rather than monumental character in architecture will not disturb but rather attract us.

One of the phenomena of present-day change is that denominational differences in liturgical practice are being blurred. This is happening as the result of the ecumenical interchanges through which the various branches of the church are learning to know each other better, and through the liturgical studies through which most Christians are seeking and finding ways to expand as well as deepen the cultic life. As a consequence of these changes two apparently opposing paths are taken. One is the path of convergence in which the common search is bringing more similarities among Christians. The tendency toward weekly eucharistic celebrations among denominations whose custom has been quarterly or monthly celebrations is an example of this, and the stronger emphasis on preaching among Roman Catholics is another. The other path is the growing openness to change and variety in worship in contrast to the use of liturgies which are fixed in detail. It is a response to particularities of place and occasion intended to bring creativity, relevance, immediacy, and vigor into the cultic experience.

Both of these characteristics were apparently present in the church in the centuries before it became a divided church — a certain framework or skeleton was generally accepted, but within this matrix there was freedom for local and sometimes extemporaneous variety in detail. The architectural implications of this kind of presupposition are not difficult to identify. If one accepts this kind of thinking he abandons, on the one hand, the supposition that places of worship ought to be alike. Local circumstances can influence rather freely the appearance, forms, and detail of the environment. There is, except for some general and obvious requirements that are easily met, no pressure to conform to an ecclesiastical vocabulary of architectural detail or of furnishings.

On the other hand, if one expects that there is to be variety responding not only to the particularities of geography, but also to the course of time, the logic of building flexible kinds of places is paramount. The currents of liturgical change are not directed now simply toward replacing the fixed forms of an earlier age with a new set of fixed forms which will hopefully congeal in better patterns. The principle now operative is that change is to be continual, and continually responsive to changes of people, occasion, and cultural circumstance — just as the liturgical practices of the early churchmen were varied and continually changing.

If the considerations of liturgy have led the worshiping community to a renewal which has a profound influence on the forms of worship spaces, other currents in the theology and piety of the Christian churches have also been flowing and must also be recognized in the forms of our structures.

The Paradigm of Incarnation

One of the fundamental elements of Christian faith which has received renewed emphasis in many ways in this century relates to the doctrine of the incarnation, and reasserts the implications of the Christmas story. The incarnation becomes the paradigm. God comes to earth, enters the human scene, acts within it. His entry becomes the hinge of history, and it teaches us that the encounter between man and God is accomplished by the act of God, not of man. The encounter takes place not because men leave their ordinary lives and proceed to a different place where God is, but because God enters their world and their lives where they are.

The stable at Bethlehem, the hillside in Galilee, the court of the Gentiles, the upper room in Jerusalem, the sidewalk cafe at Emmaus — these are the places of encounter. They are all secular places; even the temple court was secular to the Jew. We do not program God by building him a house; nor do we contain him. Furthermore, inasmuch as we are ourselves his Temple, it is the people of God who provide his presence in the world. Where they are, he is.

If we are to provide a witness to this kind of commitment in our building projects it cannot be by isolating places and ascribing to the place a particular holiness as the place of God's presence. All places are potentially the places of his presence.

It is unhappily true that as soon as people designate a place to be exclusively the place of a cultic event, the place assumes a separateness that ultimately leads to its being thought of as "holy"; and by inference other places are drained of their potentials for being places where God meets men. When this happens, as it has happened too often in the history of the church, life is compartmentalized. People no longer see that all of life is holy. They begin to think that the presence of God is localized, and begin to act as if there is a trip they must take, an effort they must make, to approach God. So "going to church" turns out to be the way to practice religion, instead of feeding and healing and teaching.

It is also unhappily true that if we give a place an architectural character that separates it from places of ordinary human concourse, by providing permanent religious symbols or liturgical devices — it is true that if we provide such a place even if we use it for other purposes, it will be thought of as a place of cult. And if this happens then the common understanding of worship becomes distorted. It is seen as something associated with certain places, instead of something which involves certain attitudes, acts, and certain kinds of people.

In the course of the last half century the movement toward building places of worship with a secular character has been more and more explicit. In this way also we are returning to the practice of the early church, and in a few instances the structures are far enough away from the traditional ecclesiasticism as to be nearly ideal. The place which is ultimately faithful to the Christian vision will be one in which the room is devoid of any explicitly cultic images or furnishings. Such a place will be prepared for the event of worship by bringing in and arranging the furnishings and accoutrements of the cult. Such a preparation becomes an event, a part of worship, and there will then be no improper association with worship as a function of place or images or things.

The Social Implications of the Gospel

One of the earliest, most controversial, and at the same time most fruitful currents of 20th century theology is what is called the Social Gospel. The prophets of the Social Gospel were persuaded that the traditional patterns of churchmanship were much less responsive to the needs of people than Jesus had been,

37

and that the character of establishment Christianity was much too like the ritual religion of Jesus' time. Whereas Jesus had spent his energies in teaching, healing, cleansing, and feeding, Christians were generally too intent on the next world, too much focused on the redemption of the individual rather than on the redemption of the world, and too much concerned with the nurture of ecclesiastical institutions and cultic formalities. While we no longer accept the naive optimism of the Social Gospel movement, we have learned to understand better the *social* implications of the gospel we preach and celebrate.

The traditional building forms of establishment churches support the criticism that the church has neglected social needs. They are other-worldly by inference, detaching themselves from the architecture of the world around them. Their triumphal monumentalism magnified the authority or the prestige of the institution, or their saccharine charm insulated their habitues from the realities of the world, or their "dim religious light" provided a sentimental and esoteric escape. Where funds were not available to erect real architecture of these qualities, imitative gestures were made in the same directions.

The social implications of the gospel have had their influence in the programs of parish activities, and therefore on buildings. The extension of the "plant" to include facilities not only for worship and teaching but for social, recreational, and even athletic activities, and for such things as day care centers, clinics, and more recently housing for the elderly, indicates that church members are more and more seeing the Christian role as the role of servanthood.

38

Ironically, those elements of a congregation's building that are devoted to service or servant functions are usually built in a forthright, real, and authentic architectural style. The "nave" or "sanctuary," presumed to be the place where the "real presence" of Christ is encountered and celebrated, is still often an architectural fantasy. The solution of this kind of unhappy contradiction is clear; the place of worship should be a place of full authenticity.

And if we are to carry the logic of the "servant church" to its undeniable end, we must proceed even further. Jesus was the "Man for others"; Christians are called to be the "men for others." Their structures should not be built unless they are directed to the service of the community of people around them and become a means for the Christian community to provide as effectively as possible not only for its own needs, but for the needs of the community.

What this ultimately means is that there can be no more church building in the sense that is meant when we talk about "houses of God," shrines, temples, naves, chancels, or sacred edifices. We need to return to the non-church.

Such a place can serve the greater community better, and can also be a better place for the Christian liturgy, than the "traditional" forms have ever been. What qualities will make it so are the subject of later pages.

3

Architecture
for 20th-Century Saints

The social convulsions of the last decade in this country have led some people to take the position that there ought to be a moratorium on church building; and even those who have not accepted this view have been earnestly trying to review the issue. Most of them have been quite willing to concede that during the 1950s and '60s the churches were investing more funds in new houses of worship and less in care for the ills of society than a proper balance would have prescribed.

The social changes seem to suggest that a change in the attitude of Christians toward building must come. They add another kind of evidence to the claim that the traditional patterns must not be carried any further. For if the building of "houses of God" is inconsistent with the essential Christian faith, its results are also damaging to society at large. This kind of activity is simply not the way a "servant church" demonstrates its "servanthood."

Back to the House Church?

What then? Shall we indeed declare a moratorium, a permanent one, and an absolute one? Is it reasonable to suppose that the churches should return to gathering in homes or other available places, abandoning the ownership of property? Everyone knows of experiments like this in communities across the country under the auspices of denominations as well as by independent congregations. To assert that these ventures have failed is a judgment no one is called on to make. To say that they have not been able to turn the patterns of church life about is fair, however. That such practices can be adopted as a general solution is unlikely. I believe that they are not even an ideal for several reasons. One is the existence of the automobile; it was possible in pedestrian days for many people to gather without troubling neighbors or making traffic problems. Another reason is that few homes these days are spacious enough to allow more than small groups to assemble. These are logistical problems which may sometimes be met, but more often cannot be.

A more valid reason is that if the church intends to minister to the world, it will often find that structures are the tools which make ministry possible. A congregation without available space is often like a carpenter without his tools.

The issue is not whether congregations own structures; it is how they conceive their structures, and how they use them. They cannot be conceived as "houses of God," places of ecclesiastical character, in distinction from places of secular character. And they must not be used exclusively for worship. In the first circumstance the implication of architectural style, in the second the implication of special use will inevitably misinform and therefore deform people. They will persist in or come to the sense that God is attached to the place rather than to the Christians.

Architecture: Technology and Art

If we choose to build then, as we may well do, what criteria ought to take the place of the traditional intentions and standards? To answer this question I should like to start by saying some things about the nature of architecture.

Architecture is both a technology and an art. As a technology it attempts to meet the demands of modern shelter, which can be complex indeed. A building needs in the first place to be organized so that the spaces within and about it are big enough for their purposes, but not too big, are shaped appropriately, arranged logically, and properly interconnected. This process is called planning. It starts with consideration of the site, the access to it, vehicular and pedestrian traffic within it, the arrangement of unenclosed spaces in relation to the enclosed structure; and it proceeds to the detail of internal spaces. It is accomplished principally by the drawing of site plans, and floor plans, but of course the vertical dimension of spaces is also involved. There is a variety of limitations that impose on the planner — zoning and building codes, exit and circulation codes, standards of space usage, such as those governing the number of cars that must be supplied a parking space, the space it takes for people to sit or move, reasonable arrangements of things like kitchen equipment and mechanical equipment.

43

The technical issues also involve problems of structures — the choice of systems and materials to meet the forces of gravity, wind, the possibilities of fire, or other disaster. The matters of temperature control, ventilation, lighting, sound, tactile, and even olfactory considerations must be considered.

Four Misconceptions About Architecture

First misconception: *good architecture consists in the skillful solution of technical problems.* This assumption is similar to one sometimes made about painting or drawing, that a kind of virtuosity in achieving a photographic likeness is a sufficient accomplishment for a painter. It is a wrong assumption because it doesn't take into account that architecture is an art as well as a technology.

For art is a means not simply of accomplishing a technical intention, but of dealing with ideas, and at its most serious, with the disclosure of truth.

In a period of several hundred years the Western world has become verbally oriented, and we have a tendency to believe that truth or knowledge is best expressed in the discursive symbol systems that are characteristic of mathematics, theology, science, and other rational disciplines. The symbol systems which mediate ideas in these categories of thought are logical and intellectual; the processes move the mind along rational paths toward conclusions that seem to be demonstrable. And there are those who have asserted that the distinguishing characteristic of the human race is the ability to deal with these abstract symbol systems.

But there is another kind of symbol system through which humans communicate, and always have, the symbol systems which communicate not through the rational intellect but through the senses, and awake the response of feeling. Music is the most obvious of these; tones, rhythms, harmonies, sequences, and other qualities of sound are the symbols which meet our sensibilities, and move us to feel as composers and performers wish us to feel. Our communication through these non-discursive methods may not be as precise as our transfer of idea and understanding through the rational verbal systems, nor can we be sure that all people respond equally or alike to the symbols. But the perceptions impinge on us at levels of consciousness that are both more obscure and more affective. And it is probably true that the ability to deal with this other kind of symbol system — which is the symbol system which artists use — is even more distinctively a human trait than is the process of reasoning.

It is almost surely true that the symbols of art are more influential in the way people behave and live, than are the rational processes. And for this reason it has been said that Bach's Passions are a better illumination of Good Friday than Anselm's or Aulen's theological treatises. For this reason the priest, who concerns himself with the ultimate order and meaning of life, and the artist, who finds affective forms to communicate that meaning, have been constant companions and sometimes the same person. And it is for this reason that Christians need to be concerned about the possibilities of art as well as theology.

We generally think of the Scriptures as verbal and belonging to the category of discursive communication; but this is to oversimplify. The Bible is not a book of systematic theology; it is more like a book of poetry, a work of art; and of Jesus' recorded words a large share, such as the parables, are metaphor rather than discursive reasoning.

Architecture then, if it is an art, is not simply technological virtuosity. There are orators who can entrance us with words—rhythms, resonance, and rhetoric—but who say nothing consequential, and there are architects with the same kind of skill. It is quite possible for excellent craftsmanship to act as a mask which by attracting attention to itself hides more valuable matter. Or it is possible that it hides no matter at all. Yet technical virtuosity is not to be deprecated. For every great artist is also a craftsman, and if he is not his art suffers. Just as the pianist trains his fingers so that he can deal with the complexities of music, and the poet learns grammar so he can write poetry, so the architect equips himself with every sort of knowledge about building so that he can devise shapes and spaces that are more than shelter. The Japanese recount the advice of an ancient artist to a younger aspirant: "Perfect your technique and wait for inspiration."

Second misconception: *the art in architecture is simply that which makes it decorative and pleasant to the senses*. The questions some people put to themselves when they encounter a new architectural form, or any new art form, are, "Do I like it? Does it please me?" The questions are the same as one asks oneself about a new flavor of ice cream or a new brand of cigar. And on reflection it seems necessary that there be some consequential difference between such trivial things and art enterprises in which wise and thoughtful people have invested their lives. It cannot be right to judge Chartres cathedral and a piece of pie by the same criteria.

We are likely to come to recognize that the works of art we admire most are not simply decorative or pretty; we value them for other reasons. Just as the persons we value most are not simply pretty or handsome but have more important qualities, the paintings, or poems, or structures we value most have more important qualities. The questions we ought to be asking are, "Does this thing convey the truth? Does it speak about something relevant and consequential?"

The Roman patrician, Vitruvius, whose books were recovered in the Renaissance, wrote that the three criteria of architectural virtue are *commoditas,* or good planning; *firmitas* or sound structure (both of these are matters of technique); and *venustas* or delight. The question of delight in art has been a perennial one among serious artists, and those who assert that art is essentially expressive or communicative are sometimes accused of being puritanical or propagandist. The fact is that most art in one way or another has been a pleasure. For the artist does not simply state what he thinks to be the truth; he celebrates it, appealing to the senses rather than the mind, or through the senses to the mind. And it is this celebration that lifts art into being art. The novelist celebrates by telling a story, and the pleasure of the tale interpenetrates and enhances the presentation of an idea. The poet celebrates with images and cadences and a dozen other sensual devices. The dramatist entertains. The decorative capital on a classic column may be thought of as the celebration of the fact that at this point the vertical shaft of the column draws in the superimposed load of the pediment above. And the pleasure of form in a suspension bridge comes from our recognition that the designer has captured and monumentalized

47

in the catenary curve an explicit image of gravitational force.

Third misconception: *architecture simply provides an exciting sensual experience.* This is not an uncommon assertion among practicing artists who often say that one should not look for meaning, but be content with a new experience; art contributes, they imply, not to making life more coherent, but simply more interesting. And a substantial amount of the work of painters, sculptors, and also of architects in this generation seems to be motivated by this view.

There is an obvious similarity in this community of thought to the attitude among the people to whom St. Paul preached on Mars hill in Athens. Luke records that they were gathered to hear "any new thing." And Paul was not very successful in preaching to them. The fault was identified in C. E. M. Joad in his book *Decadence.* A decadent society, he said, is one in which people are more attached to what is interesting than to what is true.

Yet it cannot be forbidden that a work of art should be interesting or exciting. For that which is true should by no means be dull or bland, and that which opens the horizon or helps to make the world understandable and existence coherent is not likely to be uninteresting. So it is predictable that a good piece of architecture will also be a lively experience.

Fourth misconception: *architecture is no more than a matter of self-expression.* There are those who think of art almost as psychotherapy, the occasion for the artist to vent his passions, frustrations, and idiosyncrasies. Some suppose that art is valuable because its form is especially unique, individual, and private.

48

It is scarcely to be argued that works of art are the products of the honest and personal vision of creative people, and that since people differ, the works of art must differ also. But when one deals with architecture, he works within a milieu where a complex technology is everybody's property, and this provides a certain objectivity. Materials demand certain respect, and practical problems of program are not subject to the designer's perferences, much less his whims. Furthermore, and this applies almost always to structures for institutions like churches, architecture is commissioned, and the artist owes certain loyalties to his clients' mind. So it is quite inappropriate that such buildings should be seen as the occasion for the purging of the artist's private soul. And it is not surprising that great institutional buildings of history are not idiosyncratic, that we have no records of the designers of a great many historical masterpieces, and that the best of the new church buildings are characterized, even in an age that adores "personalities," by a kind of objective restraint.

Those architects whose work is so personal as to be instantly identifiable are less likely to serve a parish well than those whose work proclaims that each project is seen as a new problem and each solution is different because the problem is inevitably different.

Architecture differs also in the medium with which the artist works, and that medium is space. LeCorbusier once said that architecture is space revealed in light. The ancient Chinese philosopher Lao Tze remarked that the important element of a cup is the void it encloses, and the same can be said of a room or any enclosure. It is, of course, a truism; but the value in stating it is not insignificant; for a great many people tend to look at buildings as masses, as if they were great pieces of sculpture, or going inside, tend to see them as a collection of surfaces, as if each were a sort of planar composition. We have not come by these tendencies dishonestly; the city scape is often a collection of facades which invite a two-dimensional appreciation, renaissance design seems frequently to be a collection of planes, and our techniques of design in which structures have been accomplished by drawing on two-dimensional paper, have influenced the thinking of designers. Masonry buildings by their very massiveness invite us to think of them as solids, rather than as voids qualified by the surfaces that limit the voids.

But if we are to suppose that people are more important than things and their activities are what make a place significant, then the void which provides for them is the starting point. And the problem of architectural design can be defined as that of giving character to the voids by the way we enclose, light, and otherwise define the voids.

Architecture as Witness

To the congregation that sets out on a building project certain questions arise or should arise that relate to the expressive character of architecture. The supposition that the institution should no longer build ecclesiastical buildings may seem to imply that the opportunity to make the architecture an expression and witness to the Christian faith has been lost. The whole tradition of church building, one may assert, has been directed toward making buildings which are vigorous and explicit witnesses to the presence of the faith in our communities. This is, after all, why the traditional churches have chosen the prominent sites in our communities; this is why the noble edifices crown the hilltops, punctuate the open spaces, lift their towers over our towns, dominate the villages. This is why the structures have been supplied with distinctive and identifiable features and details which separate them from the secular buildings surrounding them. It is precisely, one may say, because the church has been aware that architecture is an art, an art of communication, that the sixteen hundred year old tradition has been maintained. How foolish, then, to abandon it. If architecture is seen as a means of witness can we do better than our forefathers have done if we abandon the clear path they have set before us?

This is a critical issue which requires a careful answer. It is necessary to agree that those who erect structures which are taken to be the symbols of the Christian community should commit themselves to the forms which are faithful to the Christian vision, in the first place; and in the second, that the forms should communicate as lucidly as possible. If we are to be faithful we shall need to start with an examination of that which we are to be faithful to.

But before venturing into that matter, it may be fruitful to make some further comments on the relationship between structures and ideas. First let us agree on some very simple things.

The fact that Christians use a building for cultic purposes or any other purposes related to their institutional life does not therefore make it religious or Christian architecture. Nor does the fact that a Christian community owns a building make it Christian architecture. Nor does the intention of those who

51

build or the name they give to a structure make any difference. If there is any meaning in the use of the term "Christian architecture," it must derive from the quality or character of the architecture. Just as an institution is to be judged as Christian, not by its name, or its intentions, or its affiliation, but by its faithful adherence to the Christian vision, so an architectural work can be called Christian only inasmuch as it serves the work of the church, which is its ministry, and communicates faithfully the vision of the church, which is its mission.

The opportunity for service to the larger community varies so much from place to place that generalities are scarcely possible. It varies from time to time also, and the response to this fact can only be that buildings ought to be as flexible as the technology available can make them. The problem of flexibility is not unique to the church; it is part of the life of our times; and there has developed a theory of architectural design which recognizes this. Its proponents assert that structures ought to be of simple shapes, simply framed, with long spans and a minimum of permanent internal divisions. This theory is quite in contrast to the more common supposition that every varying function within a structure should be given its own particularly appropriate form. The work of Frank Lloyd Wright is most typical of this latter view; Mies Van der Rohe was the strongest exponent of the first, and their buildings take forms that are radically different as a result. Both would pay their respects to the well-known dictum "form follows function"; but the Miesians include as one of the factors of function the probability of change. The Miesian posture is obviously accepted by builders of every sort of commercial and industrial building. In varying degrees it must be seen as appro-

Exterior and plan of Unity Temple designed by Frank Lloyd Wright.

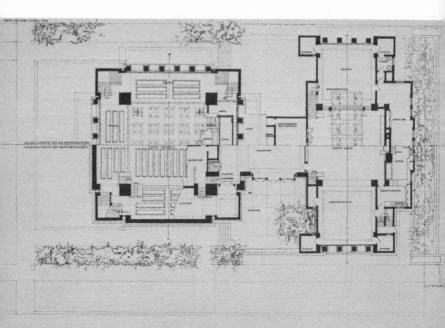

Exterior and plan of Chapel, Illinois Institute of Technology, designed by Mies van der Rohe.

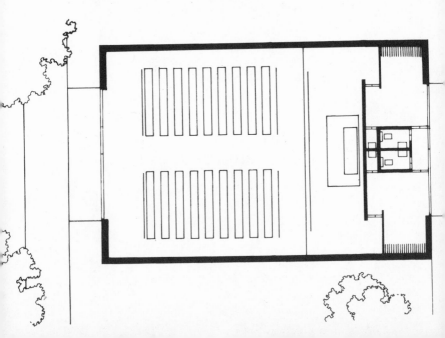

priate to churches who build also. And it is apparent that the forms and technologies which allow for change in "secular" architecture can be welcomed into the structures of the church and used most effectively if churchmen will abandon their commitment to "ecclesiastical" details and motifs.

How then, in the absence of the "ecclesiastical" details and motifs does architecture perform the mission of the church? How can it be a witness?

Let me repeat: the details and motifs have nothing to do with the matter. They are like labels, and are not the substance. They have no more to do with the matter than wearing a cross in the lapel has to do with Christian character. At best they are only a statement of intention; the reality lies elsewhere.

The reality appears in the character of the person and in the character of the architecture. It is true, for instance, that a passionately committed religious person is one who seeks always to deal with what is true and authentic. He is impatient with mere conventions, abjures masks, formalisms, illusions, artificialities, trivialities. Jesus was such a person, and his followers ought to be. The commitment to truth and to the authentic can be reflected in architecture also, and the church's architecture ought to be absolutely forthright, entirely authentic, without deceits or illusions, without artificialities of any sort.

This is a more complicated and difficult matter than it may seem to be. It means that we cannot have anything to do with the conventions of historical styles, including those conventions which are called "modern." A building with this sort of authenticity makes no attempt to seem either old or new, only to be what it needs to be. It uses materials in ways that respect their natural qualities, not distorting them for effect or disguising them. If the structure is concrete, the architect will not seek to pretend otherwise. If it is steel, the shapes will logically follow the logic of steel fabrication, and the forms will most often be straight and rectangular since these are the unaffected shapes of fabricated steel. And if it is wood, the detailing of the wood will not imitate the kind of wood structure that our forefathers used. There will be no architectural cosmetics that aim to deceive, like plaster painted to look like stone, veneered or plywood surfaces that pretend to be solid boards, plastic flooring that imitates slate or clay tile, machine-worked steel that imitates hand-wrought iron, no electric candles, plastic philadendrons, artificial leather, or wood-grained laminates. Each element, each space and substance and system of the construction, will be what it appears to be: each will be selected because it best fits its purpose and because it contributes to the logic of the whole.

Anyone who thinks this kind of authenticity comes easily or even cheaply is mistaken. Our civilization is so abundantly supplied with substitutes, artifices, artificialities, and the ersatz that the search for the genuine thing is sometimes long and expensive. Consider these further temptations. Machine-made bricks are distorted (by machine) to imitate hand-made bricks. Wood is artificially "distressed" to look old and worm-eaten. Aluminum is anodized to look like bronze. Thin asphalt shingles four feet long are segmented and colored to look like thick-butt wood shakes. Loudspeakers are mounted in plastic shells, shaped and colored to look like bells.

There are more subtle forms of affectation also: Laminated structures curve into pointed arches, not because the shape is more efficient, but because it looks "churchy." Glazed openings are so contrived and so framed as to give the illusion that no glass exists at all. Openings in walls are camouflaged to conceal their existence.

If we surround ourselves with environments of clever artifice, we cannot avoid being affected by them. We ourselves become artificial, and our capacity to live lives of authenticity is diminished.

There is some affinity between the concern a religious man has for authenticity, for being "down-to-earth," and the meaning of incarnation. Christians can learn from the Christmas story to remember that God is not found in fantasy, but that he chose to enter the world in the most earthy of circumstances. If we prepare a place for the encounter it ought to be as real as the stable, or as the Galilean hills, or the upper room in Jerusalem or the sidewalk cafe at Emmaus. Frank Kacmarcik once said when he was discussing the character of a eucharistic hall that it ought to be such that a flock of sheep could be driven through it without their seeming too much out of place. This suggests quite properly that one of the criteria we need to accept is real humility, a humility that accepts and loves the earth, that sees no need for affectations, or illusions. For if this is the character of religious people then it ought to be the character of the places they build.

There is another characteristic of religious people, particularly of Christian people, which says something about the appropriate character of their buildings.

They are said to be devoted to others. Jesus was the paragon of love, the Man for others, and his followers, if they regard his example, will make their buildings the expression of love.

This is accomplished in one way by regard to the technical matters which can help to make structures into good servants. It is more complex than this though; it is not only a matter of how a building work, but how it relates to people. History is full of appalling church buildings from this point of view, buildings which seek to dominate, buildings which overwhelm, sometimes by size, sometimes by opulence, sometimes by scale. This is so much the rule, and there is so much similarity between the structures of the church and those of temporal majesty that we Christians have made generally and for centuries the assumption that church buildings should be grand if resources allow and grandiose if they do not. And while churchmen have asserted that good people should be humble and kind, they have built churches which are presumptuous and unkind.

There are two extremes in the way buildings interact with people just as there are two extremes in interpersonal relationships. On the one hand you have the confrontation, the person who aims to dominate, who speaks in orations, who protects himself. And the architecture which represents him is the triumphal monument, the impressive edifice, the awesome temple. Not all of these structures are big, there is no need to be. The effect can be accomplished by scale or by opulence as well as by size.

At the other hand you have the open and loving human encounter where a person opens himself freely and graciously to another, with whom genuine conversation is possible. The architecture which represents him is most often domestic architecture; its keynote is hospitality. At best it cherishes people, enters into their company, and encourages them to value themselves and others. Such buildings are usually small, but are not necessarily so. Again the clue is more scale than size, together with restraint and quietness of form.

In these times, and particularly in this country, where advertising art has a strong influence on all of design including the design of buildings, a particular kind of temptation is present. It is true perhaps that power and authority are not the symbols that designers value these days, but the approach of the advertising artist is not less destructive; his aim is to manipulate people by whatever subtle devices are available. He aims to attract, and he attracts by cleverness, surprise, and a kind of slickness and gloss; and his art appeals to us on a level which is often seductive, almost always superficial, and not infrequently deceitful. We have learned to distrust the advertiser because we suspect he really doesn't love us. He wants to use us. A good deal of architectural design has caught the disease.

The designers of church buildings have not been immune. An assumption was expressly articulated and broadly accepted some years ago that the aim of ecclesiastical architecture was first to attract and then to seduce people into what was called the "mood of worship," by whatever manipulative devices could be invented. This usually meant mood music, elements of spectacle, dramatic lighting devices, rich and soft color, luxurious seating, carpeted quietness, and

59

sonorous rhetoric. The goals of this syndrome, as we look back on it, seem to have been much more those of manipulative psychology than of uncovering the truth. It was a comparatively mild process, but its similarity to the inhuman techniques of brainwashing are obvious. This kind of huckster approach to religion has now been criticized sufficiently, but it has not yet disappeared. And the kind of architecture which supported it still appears.

The Place of Beauty

This discussion on the appropriate character of the architecture of church members, has dealt so far with the hope that their buildings might be expressions of the Christian concern for what is real and true, and that they might also communicate that sort of love which is a reflection of God's love. Predictably perhaps, these paragraphs need to be joined by some comments on the quality of beauty, for the beautiful thing and the religious vision form a unique relationship.

In his classic, *The Idea of the Holy,* Rudolf Otto distinguishes between three aspects of the religious consciousness. One of these is that search for reality which is called philosophy or metaphysics or theology and concerns itself with the conceptual nature of truth. A second is the ethical sensibility, the awareness and commitment to what is good. Though both of these matters are closely related to religion, they are not its unique and distinctive quality. This unique quality is not subsumed under the categories of either metaphysics or ethics, but is something different, namely the idea of the holy, or the numinous. It is the human awareness that our lives are lived in the presence of a magnificent mystery — awesome, fascinating, ineffable. It is this transcendent mystery which is the holy.

The experience of the numinous comes to us all. It is not alone the property of poets and mystics. We are led to it when we reflect on such intimate and immanent things as the wonder of the heart beat or the unfathomable properties of time or the space in which we exist.

Though we are surrounded by this *mysterium tremendum,* we find it quite impossible to deal with it in rational and discursive processes. We can point to it but we cannot analyze it, factor it, synthesize, or systematize it. And all our attempts to deal with it logically fail to bring us close. Indeed they seem to mask it and even estrange us from the holy.

But one of the enterprises in which men engage has the power to meditate the numinous; this is the work of art. And this is no doubt why Andre Maurois could write, "All art in its origin was religious, and religion has often found in art the means of communicating to the human consciousness truths which the intelligence can discover only with difficulty."

For the beautiful is also a sort of mystery. Like the numinous it also refuses to be factored, codified, or synthesized by the faculties of logic. Like the numinous it merely presents itself, and we are moved to a sort of wonder. The beautiful thing, whether a sky full of stars or a tea cup, can open for us portals to a consciousness not merely of delight, but of the most profound awe, and awake a sort of yearning.

This is why the esthetic and the religious belong together, and have been together in history. And this is why it is utterly wrong if those structures which a Christian community erects should be prosaic or commonplace or banal or ugly. And this is why a congregation that intends to build, no matter what it builds, must set its mind to engaging the best of artistic skills, architectural and otherwise, to serve its purposes.

Architecture Beyond the Church Building

What has been said about the architecture of the Christian community is entirely applicable to the architecture for which Christian people take responsibility in their lives outside of the institutional church — their homes, their shops, schools, and whatever else they build. For if the structures we erect in behalf of the church can take on a character which is both non-ecclesiastic and at the same time seriously religious, no less or more ought to be expected of all the structures religious people control. And if we really see our faith as something that comprehends all of life, and not just the cultic event, then there can be no difference in the criteria by which we assess architectural form, except those criteria which relate to the infinite variety of physical functions.

This turns out to be an immense challenge. The burden of change in our communities that ought to result from accepting such a responsibility extend far beyond the possible changes to the environments in which we worship. But if the Kingdom of God is to come among us can we deny the need for change? If Christians accept the idea that all their actions in all their days should witness to their faith, all of their architecture must also witness.

This view of architecture is consistent with the gospel. The gospel sets us free from the religion of ritual laws and temple worship, but presents the more demanding imperative of loving behavior; this view of architecture sets us free from the formalities and fixed proprieties of ritual architecture, but presents us with the imperative of bringing all the environment into the realm of the religious.

The End of the Cathedral?

If the place of worship must no longer be the majestic monument of former years, will we not impoverish people? For these noble edifices are a glory of human history that has enriched generation after generation. Shall we have no more cathedrals? Shall we doom ourselves to the small, the moderate, what one might even call trivial?

There are two answers to this concern. One is that great architecture, despite our heritage, is not necessarily magnificent, oratorical, and overwhelming. To deprecate St. Peter's Cathedral as a work of art is to be blind; but the Katsura Villa, which is as humane as St. Peter's is pompous, as gracious as St. Peter's is domineering, and as lovely as St. Peter's is magnificent, represents one of the alternatives. It would be a better image of the Christian community despite its being Japanese.

The second answer is that there is no reason to suppose large structures or complexes would disappear. But if Christians who see their opportunities are in control, the large structures will be as kind as they are large and as gently scaled as smaller structures. And though they will not be thought of as ecclesiastical buildings, they may very well be the meeting places of congregations and may even be owned by them. So the human race will not be impoverished but made richer by the change.

Sacred and Secular Art

What has been said about the architecture of faith can be applied in principle to the other visual arts as well, to sculpture and painting and all their variations, to the design of artifacts and the larger environmental arts. We should be open, for instance, to the possibility that the common distinction between so called "religious" painting and sculpture, which is usually seen as related to the iconographic subject matter, is an illusion. For many people this has long been clear. A generation or more ago it was pointed out that Leonardo's "Last Supper," despite its being cherished as a religious image, carries no consequential religious insight; it is a very skillful and perceptive illustration of a dramatic instant in the life of Jesus, exhibiting psychological understanding but no passion of faith. Conversely, Paul Tillich noted that Picasso's tortured mural on the bombing of Guernica might well be called religious because it is as searing a comment on hatred and inhumane warfare as the utterance of an Old Testament prophet. (Its beauty, incidentally, could hardly be termed delightful.)

Since there are no boundaries between the sacred and the secular in the life and architecture of the Christian, all of experience having been seen to be potentially sacred, then all things beautiful may be seen as portals to the transcendent and many works which include no specifically ecclesiastical image may illuminate the religious consciousness.

And we will no doubt discover that places and building that we had thought to be secular are in fact more congenial to the gathering of the cultic community than most of our existing church buildings, because they are at once more authentic, more hospitable, and more beautiful.

4

Designing
the Centrum

I propose not an adventure into an unknown country, but a return to the land of the early church where we should have been all the time. And our trip back is by now not a long one. We need not reconstruct in these days and this world the exact circumstances of the church in the Roman Empire. It seems futile, for instance, to assert that our churches should meet in homes as a consistent pattern, since to do so would require a fracturing of our congregations. To say that they should meet in other available places, like public schools, theaters, college and university auditoriums, as a permanent practice is also futile. Such places rarely provide a congregation with either the kind of facilities that best serve the parish life or the freedom of schedule and use that a parish needs.

If a parish has the freedom to own property and the sense of servanthood and public responsibility that Christians ought to have, it is likely that the parish will find a structure of some sort not only a useful medium of service, but an urgent need.

To catalog these possible opportunities is not here required; each community will have its own combination of needs ranging from schools, child care, and youth centers, to cultural centers and possibly even shops and restaurants.

In any event the structure is not to be a church; it is a place through which the church can minister. Its location will likely be established in consideration of effective ministry, and the sites may not be much different from some of those now selected, where the choice is governed by accessibility, economy, and other practical considerations.

The Centrum

Somewhere in whatever complex the parish plans there should be a space of generous size, big enough for the liturgical celebrations of the community. For although every part of a church's structure, and every structure built by churchmen, ought to be informed by and be a reflection of Christian commitments, it is in the liturgical event that the Christian vision is most clearly and most fully articulated. And it should be in the space used for the liturgy that the architectural and visual image of the church appears most lucidly and most completely.

Let me repeat: this does not mean that the room is a "nave," a "sanctuary," a "eucharistic hall," or that it should have any ecclesiastically connotative title at all. It is a meeting place for people. It will be so different a thing from the usual "church" that any of these terms which carry the sense of special purpose liturgical centers is inappropriate. A word like *centrum* may be sufficiently free of ecclesiastical connotations to be useful.

68

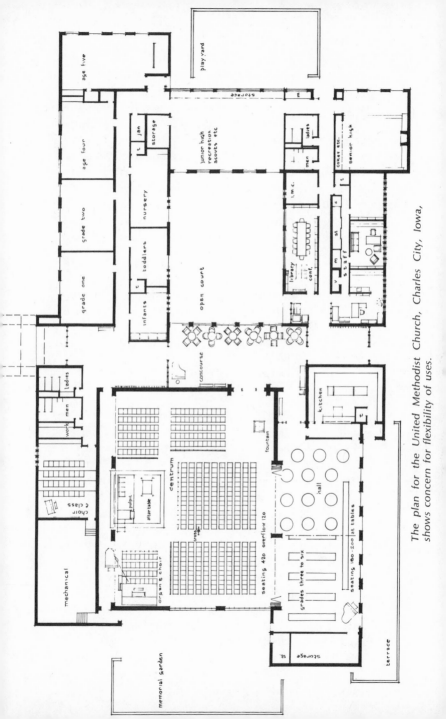

The plan for the United Methodist Church, Charles City, Iowa, shows concern for flexibility of uses.

A centrum then is a place for more than one purpose, and must be so seen, and so used. If it is not, if for one reason or another it is reserved for the liturgy, it will sooner or later be thought of as the "house of God"; and then it will be thought of as the holy place; and then other places will be seen as profane or secular; and then we shall again be denying what the church really believes. But if we can keep the centrum as a multi-purpose space into which the liturgical event is brought from time to time, some good things will happen.

In the first place, we may be reminded that the Christian community is a pilgrim community that has no certain resting place. The centrum will be our "tent," not our fortress. We gather provisionally. Our life is contingent.

In the second place, we may hope that the church can supply the comfort of permanence in a world of change.

If the architectural spaces and forms are of sufficiently high quality, they will not become archaic and obsolete. It is true that many of our buildings are dated, that we find them tiresome and disagreeable because they are so intractable a product of an earlier time. But this is not simply the fault of age; it is the fault of poor design in the first place. It is not age that has made such buildings bad; they were never really good even when they were new. There are buildings equally "dated" which we treasure and use with joy, because they are good architecture, and they will always be good. And it should be our aim to build so well that age will not bring obsolescence to our structures but add to their virtues, as age has added value to the best work of our forefathers.

This "concourse" serves as a foyer and as a meeting room.

Meanwhile we shall offer in a good centrum the opportunity for change of innumerable kinds. For the space itself must be simple, allowing for many configurations of use. And the furnishings and symbolic devices will be portable, so they may be varied, replaced, augmented or abandoned as the parishioners of future times desire.

The multipurpose space will have this virtue too, that its use will be more intense. There is no adequate reply to those who criticize the churches today because they have invested their money in monuments that are used only by themselves and only for a few hours a week.

To say a room needs to be multipurpose is not to say it needs to serve every imaginable purpose. If it is to be used effectively for liturgical events, however, there are many other intentions it can meet, and the common base among these functions must be that they deal with people. So the room will be seen as a shelter for *people,* not for machinery or things. So conceived it must be emphatically secular in character, but it must not be dull or bland or a minimum and unimaginative container. If it is for people, its scale and proportion, its articulations, its textures, colors, acoustic qualities, its provisions for ventilation and temperature control — all these details of architectural design — need to be designed for people.

If it is to serve as a place for music, it may need to be especially carefully designed acoustically, perhaps with means of varying the acoustic properties as concert halls have.

If it is to be used for theatrical events, considerations for lighting and staging and other theatrical ancillaries need to be made. If it is to be used for cinema, projection facilities will be required, and it may be fruitful to explore the use of rear-screen projection since such devices do not require a darkened room and therefore provide a flexibility not found in the usual cinema.

If it is to be used as a place where food is served, adjacencies to a kitchen or at least a caterer's facility will be required.

One important element in any multipurpose room is convenient storage space. Partitions devices may be required if the intended uses prescribe them. Flexible public address systems where input and speaker locations can be changed without elaborate inconvenience may be useful.

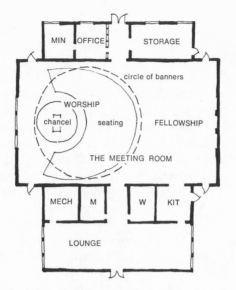

A single major space serves a great variety of purposes.

Liturgical Space

Having said this much about the alternate uses of the "centrum," which may well be the primary ones, we examine the reasonable demands of the liturgy. When people gather in an open space to listen to a soap-box orator, the shape of the assembly is likely to fall into a mass that is rough circular, with the speaker at one point on the edge or slightly inside the edge. Since speaking and reading are parts of the liturgy, this provides one clue to a reasonable shape. When people gather in activities of interchange and interaction, the normal shape is likewise a circle, but if there is a moderator or presider, the shape is likely to be more like a half-circle. If we think of a family reunion, we assume a circle or gathering at a hearth. For a meal we like to think of a round table, but if the group is large and the ·food is more refreshment than meal, people may move to and away from the table, or the food and drink may be distributed to them. In large receptions or parties the large mass normally subdivides itself.

From these observations we can make some generalizations about a good liturgical space. It should be one space. Its horizontal proportions should not be too much elongated (perhaps a length of two times the breadth is an absolute upper limit). It should not necessarily be a space absolutely clear spanned, but if there are internal columns they should be thoughtfully located.

The room need not be entirely a flat floor, but sloping surfaces are rarely possible because they are inflexible, and if terraced floor surfaces are used, they should be carefully planned so as not to inhibit flexible use and arrangements. Balconies or galleries may be wise in large centrums. In rooms to accommodate five or six hundred or fewer balconies may be economically unsound, and in smaller centrums may require that the ceiling height be higher than would otherwise be desirable. Codes now generally require two access paths to balconies with room for more than 30 people, and since stairways are expensive, this may counsel against loft spaces. There is also the other question: can groups of people on separate levels be so related that they sense their unity? Perhaps in large spaces where any intimate sense of community is attenuated anyway, the containing volume can be diminished by the use of balconies, and this can compensate for other losses.

We are all aware that on the printed page certain margins and other "white space" contributes to the grace of the graphic organization. In a similar manner open spaces in any place of assembly contribute to

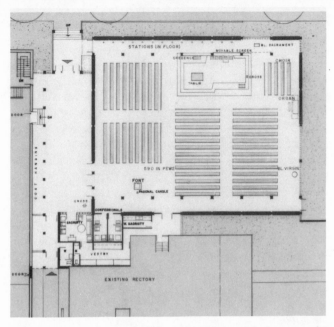

Although pews and a fixed platform limit somewhat the non-cultic uses, generous marginal spaces increase the sense of hospitality.

the grace of its confines and reduce its stiffness. A room or an arrangement that leaves only minimum aisles and clear areas should therefore be avoided. As a rule of thumb it is appropriate to supply a total space of about 15 sq. ft. for each seat.

The marginal space is necessary in the vertical dimension also. Schemes which attempt to reduce the ceiling heights to minimums because artificial light and ventilation no longer require high vaults are inevitably disagreeable. Vault heights of exaggerated dimensions like the medieval may not be required, but the vertical dimension supplies qualities for the senses, and high ceilings ennoble any activity they shelter. Furthermore the quality of music is diminished if sound has no space to resonate.

The design tradition we have inherited from the Renaissance has led us to assume that every large room should be organized symmetrically, and we tend to look for some dominating feature about which the room comes to focus. This is almost always the approach amateur designers take; it is easy and safe. But if one starts with the assumption that a room is to have several possibilities of use and arrangement, any strong axial symmetries may be troublesome, and if we declare that *people* are really the focus of what happens in the liturgy (or in any other people-oriented activities) then any very strong architectural focus can subvert our intentions. In the liturgy, furthermore, the focus normally ought to move from one place to another. The pulpit is logically the focus of the space when it is occupied; the table is the reasonable focus during the Eucharist. A choir ought to be prominent if it contributes special music. The place of baptism should, when this rite takes place, be the focus of the room. And there are times, such as the singing of hymns, when the total community should be the focus.

To think about the liturgical event and the liturgical room this way is rather sharply different from the patterns we have inherited. But there are some good prototypes for this conception, so one need not be fearful.

The most interesting prototype may be that of the Japanese tea house. To think of such a place as an analog for a place of Christian worship may be surprising; to those who know the tea ceremony and its environment the analogy will be clear. The tea ceremony is at best a ritual aimed at human interaction at the most profound level of openness and seriousness. It must be enough to say here that the places prepared for these events are beautiful and simple, elegant and earthy, assymetric, inventive, and altogether gracious.

There is another analogy closer to home. Not many of the living-dining rooms in our new homes can match the tea rooms for loveliness, but they are usually bigger at least and more familiar. A moment of reflection will recall to any of us assymetrical and hospitable rooms, so organized that the focus can move from hearth, to piano, perhaps to a window, to a dining table, and perhaps to other things as the activity of the people within the room shifts.

As I have suggested earlier the arrangement for worship ought to avoid the scheme in which one has the sense of a stage-audience, and equally that of the arena. The liturgical actions together with the liturgical furniture ought to be distributed throughout the room as possible. For instance, the place of baptism need not be near the table and pulpit; candles or torches, if they are used, need not be on or even near the table; flower bouquets or other decorative greenery can be placed otherwise than at the eucharistic center; banners or other symbolic devices can be placed so that they surround rather than confront the congregation. The intent of the organization is to suggest that there is no longer a "nave"; it is all "chancel."

Pews or Chairs?

Nothing gives the conventional church building its ecclesiastical character more than do pews, and nothing inhibits flexibility more than pews.

Pews are said by their advocates to have these virtues in comparison with chairs: They are orderly (but

In this centrum only organ and fountain are fixed in place.

chairs, when they are linked together are orderly also). They supply accommodations for hymnbooks (but in doing so they take on an ecclesiastical character; furthermore some chairs also are equipped with book boxes). They can easily be equipped with kneelers (but chairs can be supplied with hassocks if the liturgy requires kneeling). Pews are also said to be less expensive; and they usually are. But the difference in cost is not a big factor.

Chairs have the advantages of great flexibility. They can be arranged in various patterns, spaced freely or tightly to meet the number of people assembled. Although the fire-safety laws in most places require that chairs be interlocked in places of assembly, the principle limitation this sets on their use is the necessity of arranging them in straight rows. Yet even this is not an absolute requirement; the interlocks on some available chairs allow for curved rows. The flexibility of chairs is not more important than their scale in comparison to pews. If one aims at providing something like domestic scale, one of the surest paths to defeat is to use pews.

The least expensive chairs are of metal or metal-and-plastic. Some of these are well designed and relate comfortably to some environments. Some chairs designed especially for church buildings attempt to bridge between chair and pew: when they are interlocked they resemble pews. Such an artifice should be avoided; it is an attempt to keep one foot in the country of the ecclesiologists. A number of available chairs give the option of upholstered seats and backs; aside from the comfort and the opportunity for color and texture it provides, an upholstered surface has an acoustic virtue. The soft surfaces absorb some sound

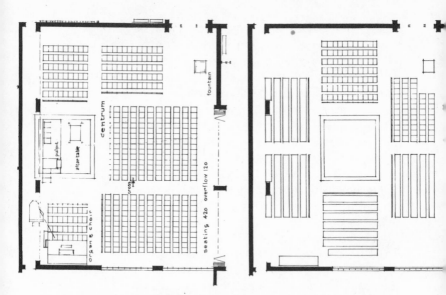

Alternate seating arrangements for centrum of United Methodist Church, Charles City, Iowa.

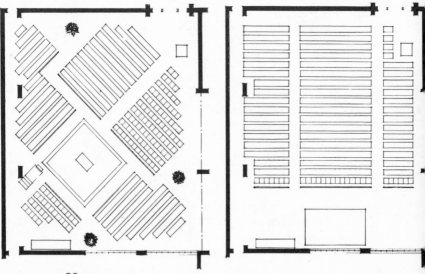

when unoccupied, and thus the acoustic difference between a full or an empty room is diminished.

Chairs used in flexible-use situations need to be easily
stored, and therefore should be designed for folding
or stacking. Most codes for seating require a minimum
seat spacing of 18 inches per person and minimum
row spacing of 32 inches. Such minimums are really
minimums; good planning provides 20 or 21 inches
and 36 inches. When such dimensions are used, it is
generally possible to augment the seating for festival
occasions by reducing the back-to-back spacing and
setting up an extra row or two.

The Platform

In truly flexible spaces a raised platform should not be
a permanent structure any more than seating should
be permanent. In small rooms where there are fewer
than six rows, a platform may not be a necessity at
all, but this is not a common situation. Yet it should
be recognized that the intent of a dais or platform is
not to accent a "sanctuary" as separate from the containing space. It is simply to provide enough elevation
so that certain liturgical functions which need visibility
get it. A platform high enough for this and big enough
so that the furniture and movements related to the
liturgical actions are comfortably managed is what is
required. If the platform is too much elevated or too
large, its height and size will tend to imply a more
than functional distinction between the members of
the community and the sense that this place is of particular sanctity.

Perhaps it is worth noting that the eucharistic table,
since the gestures and words that are related to the

A platform of modular panels can be moved and assembled in various configurations.

Eucharist are mostly a familiar ritual, need not be as clearly visible as the place of reading and preaching, and therefore need not be as high. Readers and speakers profit more from clear visibility. The leaders of prayer need no particular visibility at all; the sound of the voice is sufficient, since prayers are not commonly accompanied by gesture or other eye-directed expression. There is indeed no reason why prayers need to be led from an elevated position providing they can be heard well; and there is good reason why many of the prayers can be read from positions more intimately associated with the total body of believers; they are, after all, not personal but common prayers.

A platform may also be the location appropriate to the presider's seat and for seating for his assistants. This is a reasonable physical relationship. A case can be made, however, for seating those who minister with the body of the congregation, since during parts of the liturgy, such as the confession, they are not distinguished from the total community. And their ascension to the platform is logical only for the performance of liturgical functions that require it.

A platform, if it is to serve temporary uses and be movable, must be carefully designed for this intention. In most circumstances this will mean that it should be made of modular units. These units should be of a size and weight to be handled by one person or at most two. They should be stable, simple, durable, and good looking. A good platform should be such that its size and shape can be changed to serve a variety of purposes and locations. The same platform units ought to be available for non-liturgical uses, perhaps as staging for dramatics and for musical events. Modular units made of timber, rather than plywood, with interlocking devices and weighing not more than sixty or seventy pounds make sense. And if possible all units should be alike and interchangeable. No such modules are currently prefabricated; but like other elements of structure and furnishings they can be custom built.

The Eucharistic Table

The eucharistic table is usually called an altar, but ought to be distinguished (as it was by the early Christians) from the sacrificial altars of other religions. Its genus is rather the genus of the dining table. It is the table at which a ritual meal is served, and its symbolic value is like that of the dining table in the home. It stands for unity, fellowship, the intimate companionship of a family.

If it is to carry this symbolic burden, its location and

Altar table, human-scaled and portable.

its form must be such as to support the symbolic intent. And it is clear that some of our heritage in the history of ecclesiastical architecture must be abandoned. The history is one of diverse forms. Something has been made of the apparent use in the catacombs of the tops of sarcophagi as table tops to support the use of casket-like altars. The development of the cult of martyrs led to the erection of altars over martyrs' graves, to the occasional entombment of martyrs' remains within the altar structure itself, and to the convention of providing at least a cavity for a relic within the altar. Inevitably this kind of practice led away from the wood table to elaborated stone altars, and to the aggrandizement of the altar by providing decorative settings of great magnificence where numerous relics could be deposited.

Under these circumstances the form of a table was lost; so also was the basilican location, in which the table stood free in space at a location forward of the apse. The basilican posture could not be maintained, and although it is possible to defend the custom of the celebrant turning away from the nave on the ground that this eastward facing unified priest and people in the orientation of prayer, it has indisputable symbolic faults. The altar is no longer conceived of as a table; it is removed from the people and seems to become the property of the clergy; the speech and actions of the eucharistic liturgy are not readily seen and heard; the piece of furniture is no longer designed as furniture but as building, and thus its shapes and proportions are no longer as clearly related to the human being.

History supplies other patterns of considerable variety. The sixteenth century Reformation led to the removal of the medieval altars and reliquary adjuncts from many church buildings. One pattern adopted by Lutherans set a table lengthwise in the former choir, where the participants in the mass could gather all around it. Another pattern brought the table down into the nave, and though Luther was cautious about wholesale changes in the patterns of worship, he did express himself in favor of the basilican posture. Other reformers were more radical. Calvin himself wished to retain the weekly Eucharist, but his followers generally did not, and prevailed. The altars were removed from the churches of the Calvinist tradition, and the celebration of communion involved setting up temporary tables. In England for a period, a clear conception of the Eucharist as meal rather than sacrificial event was sought, and a law was passed (but not consistently followed) which prescribed that the table should be of ordinary wood and design and not heavier than could be carried by two men.

When one sifts through history and considers the present situation, I think he comes to these conclusions: The eucharistic table ought to be located where it can be sensed as belonging to the whole gathered community, which means that it must not be remote. It ought to be a table; not something else like a box or a pedestal. The basilican posture ought to be normal, as it is already among Roman Catholics. So that the celebrant should not be obscured by it, and that it be understood as a table, its height ought to be about 30 inches rather than 40 or more, as was the former convention. There is a minor difficulty in this height: it is hard for some celebrants to read a book lying flat on a table-height surface. Rather than raise the whole table top to avoid this, the book ought to be raised on a book rest or cushion. Other objects on the table should probably be limited to those necessary for the ritual. There is no reason for not having candles and flowers on the table, as we do on our tables in our homes, except that they may confuse the setting for ritual objects, and obscure visibility. Candles may well be floor-standing, and flowers may be set in many places. And if the table is to be portable it should not be very large.

One may have inferred from some earlier pages that the communion rail is an unnecessary ecclesiastical device. I want here to state this clearly: it is not only unnecessary, it is a handicap. Its origins are obscure. Some say it was originally a fence to keep dogs away. Some say the practice of kneeling for communion, despite its popularity in the "liturgical" denominations, goes only as far back as Louis IX in France. At its best the communion rail has been seen as a convenient extension of the altar, and some covered it with a white table cloth to make this evident. At its worst it has been a fence intentionally dividing the people from the clergy. In effect it always does this and should be avoided for this reason. But an equally good reason is that the posture of kneeling for communion contributes to the general attitude that the Eucharist is essentially a penitential and individualistic event. This view diminishes the meanings of the words "celebration" and "communion." A celebration ought to be joyful, but kneeling is not the posture of joy; in a communion one ought to be particularly conscious of the community, who together participate in Christ; but kneeling is not a posture in which we can properly commune. The Eucharist is not a private ritual; it is something shared. Even when the Eucharist is given privately, as to the sick, it is intended to be the warrant of the individual's participation in a community of Christians.

There are images we can borrow from secular life: the family meal for small groups, and for larger ones perhaps the reunion reception, the banquet, and parties of various sorts. The procession which has become the rule in Catholic churches where the Eucharist is given standing is surely an improvement on kneeling. But the best celebration of which I have been a part was one where the distribution was much less a routine, and the members of the parish took the occasion to greet each other, introduce each other, and declare to each other their joy in many ways. The room swarmed for a few minutes, and the mood was one of warmth and thanksgiving and love.

The Pulpit

In a small room a table with a book rest can also serve as a place for reading and for preaching. This will probably not be the best circumstance in a larger room where better positions may be found or a higher elevation may be desirable for the proclamation and exposition of the Word. It is true that in some of the most ancient churches the preaching was from the elevated chair of the bishop. There were no pews or chairs for the people; presumably they sat on the floor or stood where they could see and hear best. In later times highly elevated ambos or pulpits were provided. Their height was established by the long distances, or in later times because the preacher had to speak to people in flat-floored galleries.

Doubtless the elaboration of the pulpits and their height was also a reflection of the importance ascribed to the proclamation of the divine Word. And it is not surprising that in times when grand and pompous gestures, generally accompanied authority, the places of proclamation in church buildings were somewhat pompous. Today when the president of the country speaks to the citizens in a business suit from a chair behind a desk, it seems a little unreal to build towers for preachers. And indeed it may be unreal even to fix a particular place for preaching. The style of oratory appropriate to the grand lectern or pulpit seems to have passed. Many preachers find that they can communicate more effectively if they have the freedom to move about, and the use of portable microphone systems gives this freedom.

In any event, liturgical furniture that is portable and flexible allows for the *ad hoc* solution. The place of preaching should fit the preacher. And when a parish changes pastors, there need be no hesitation in making changes in the liturgical adjuncts.

Acoustics

Acoustic aids also serve the preacher. In a room of less than 100,000 cubic feet no general amplification should be needed. Under the best conditions a person with a good voice will need no amplification even in a much larger space. There are a few simple things that anyone involved in the form of worship spaces ought to know about acoustic design. Speech is best understood in rooms where there is not much resonance; music on the other hand, sounds best in resonant spaces. In both circumstances the resonance should be about the same for high, medium, and low-pitched sounds. Amplifying systems are not the sure cure for acoustic problems; and whenever a voice is filtered through an electronic system there is some loss of the person-to-person quality that makes for really human communication. An amplifier is like an overcoat. It is not an advantage but sometimes a necessity, and ought to be avoided when possible.

It is sometimes possible to avoid an electronic speaker system by using a sounding board over a pulpit. To be effective this needs to be a fairly heavy plane. It should be horizontal or nearly so, and the lower it is, the smaller it needs to be. It is an ancient device but often a good one.

Even when a liturgical room is acoustically good enough not to require general amplification, it makes sense to provide for the hard-of-hearing by the device of a radiating loop (usually in the floor) through which aural receivers can be stimulated. And since microphones and amplifiers will be required for this, it makes some sense also to allow for sound recording.

Where an audio speaker system is required, the design

of such a system should consider not only the various configurations possible in liturgical events, but also for what other activities may occupy the space. This may mean that several plugs for microphones and speakers should be distributed about so that long cables or wiring can be avoided. Speakers may be mounted on standards which can be moved from place to place. Microphones and speakers are now commonly accepted items of furniture in our places of public assembly; there is no point in trying to conceal them, but their appearance should be a matter of concern.

A serious consideration of the flexible uses of a space may well lead to a much more complex problem in acoustical quality. The conventional approach to the design of the acoustic character of places of worship has been to recognize that both music and speech with their divergent acoustical needs must take place in the room because liturgy involves both. Having recognized this, most responsible designers compromise between the hopes of the speaker and those of the musicians. The larger a room is, the less satisfactory such a compromise is likely to be. In concert halls and some other public places where people are less willing to accept compromise, it has become a common practice to provide systems of movable baffles, curtains, or other devices so that the acoustic quality of a room can be changed to fit the desires of performers and audience. This kind of device is expensive and has rarely been used by those who design for churches. But I think that if a congregation intends to provide a room which can be used not only for liturgical functions but for other public events, it must undertake what is required to make a place good acoustically. Otherwise it will stand empty more than it should.

A more recent solution to the desire for acoustical flexibility is accomplished through a very complex electronic system referred to as acoustic enhancement. The principle of this system is to build a room which is acoustically "dry" or non-resonant (which is normally good for speech). Resonance appropriate to music is then introduced by picking up the music at its source through microphones, extending the duration of tones electronically, and distributing these extended tones through a great many speakers scattered about the room. This system is being used in a number of concert halls, including London's Festival Hall. But its cost is very high at present.

Visual Projection

The development of acoustic engineering into a science (albeit not a very exact science) has given to the architects of public places some opportunities our grandfathers didn't have, at the cost of adding a very complex new technology to the province of architecture. At about the same time another new technology has also been added, the technology of visual projection for stills and moving pictures. If a church can provide a good place for cinema, it has an additional way of serving a community and making a building more useful. Furthermore, some pastors appreciate and use projection facilities as part of worship. If the rooms we worship in were more accommodating, perhaps there would be more of them.

Obviously an almost universal handicap is that projection facilities are crude if they are available at all, and another is that places of worship are usually too light for conventional projection systems. The alternative to the fussiness of blackout curtains is the use of a rear-screen system which, like the TV set, does not require a dark room. This is a common enough device in worship space specially designed for the deaf and mute people, as it is in educational and commercial institutions. There is a rigid limitation at present because the available screen size is uncomfortably small for rooms holding more than about four hundred people.

An increasing amount of good cinematic material is being produced by competent and imaginative people for use by churches, and the visual technology is likely to become more and more a part of liturgical or paraliturgical activity in American parishes.

But the visual presentation is a complex technology. Americans see enough skillful work on the screens of cinemas and television sets so that anything hastily thrown together by amateurs is likely to make the whole enterprise seem trivial.

The Lectern

It has been a convention in most churches to install a lectern in addition to a pulpit. Sometimes it has been supplied to provide visual symmetry about a central axis. The constraints of this kind of design are no longer a burden to architects. Sometimes it has been considered the place where laymen may read or speak, while the special dignity of the pulpit has been reserved for the clergy. A certain doctrine of the office of the ministry has validated this custom; and where this doctrine holds, a lectern is likely to be needed. The lectern should be placed where it is most useful without regard to bilateral symmetry.

A third pattern in the provision of a lectern is that which refers to a church as having a gospel side and an epistle side (the lectern being the epistle side and the pulpit on the gospel side). This convention reflects the strictures of bilateral symmetry and has its roots in the traditions that referred to the central altar as the "throne of Christ," and saw all the features of the ecclesiastical building as related to this position. In the days when the tabernacle with the reserved sacrament was located on or at the altar (in Roman Catholic and Anglican practice), the phrase and the conception was reasonable enough. Current practice makes it archaic. Since tabernacles are ideally outside the eucharistic halls, there is no longer reason to use language that implies that any object is the center around which the space is given order.

Lecterns, then, need not be considered essential, and if one is needed, its location and form need follow only the requirements of function and good design.

Baptismal Furniture

One starting point for the design of liturgical furnishings is clearly the matter of function. A table, for instance, needs a flat surface big enough and high enough from the floor. A lectern needs a sloping surface of another size at another distance from the floor. When one asks about the furniture for baptism the function is harder to bring into focus. Is the baptismal vessel a pool or a lavatory? Is the event an ablution or a plunge? For one sort of event it is easy to deal with portable and even changeable utensils—a basin or bowl, and a pitcher or pail to fill it. The bowl can be set on the table or on a pedestal or held by a person, filled with water beforehand or during the ritual.

Fountain near the centrum entrance may be used for baptisms.

The place of the ritual can be at the doorway as befits the sacrament of initiation, or on the platform, or at another convenient place.

If the rite is seen as a plunge, the matter of providing a pool is more troublesome, since pools are not portable. But the matter is not very hard in any event. Some of the most pleasant amenities in public rooms all over the world are fountains of running water. They are not "fonts" (which is one of the ecclesiastical words we may just as well forget), and many of the fountains we know are much finer symbols of cleansing than the fonts in most of our churches.

If the place for worship is a place of assembly for other events, as a centrum is likely to be, a permanent feature can be a fountain built into a wall or free standing—a feature that is as much an asset to the room during "secular" uses as it is useful for the baptismal rite. Warming the water if required, is not a difficult problem. The question whether or not to recirculate water depends on the amount of flow designed.

There are several good reasons for setting such a device near the entrance to the centrum. Water, especially if it is even slightly in motion, gives a hospitable welcome. This is enhanced even more if plants and flowers are present. At the entrance such a feature will probably interfere less with flexible uses of a space than at any other place. For those to whom the fountain will be a reminder of the baptismal sacrament the place of coming and going is a good place. Those whose usages include holy water stoups may well be able to get along without them if the water of an entrance-way fountain is allowed to serve the same purpose. The presence of a fountain doesn't require that it be used for the baptismal ritual, but at least it can be. When it is, the rite can include such a gesture as having everyone stand and turn—a gesture that may get more people more involved in the rite than they are when it is performed in front of the seated. The objection to this location, and it has some weight, is that it is difficult for people to see the ceremony. This is true, but it is also often true when it takes place in front of the people. One usually depends on hearing to follow the stages of the ceremony—not on vision.

These comments imply that the scheme of the centrum brings people into the room at some point behind the chairs. I should not want to suggest that this is necessary; if people enter otherwise, other possibilities and problems appear.

The location of the baptismal celebration is not as important as the action that surrounds it, or as expressive. No room and no arrangement of a room is going to serve its symbolic purposes well, unless the action of the liturgy exploits the space. For instance, if a typical font stands before a congregation, the bowl being full of water ahead of time, and a baby, family and sponsors seated ten feet away, so that almost nothing of any visual impact happens, and the ceremony is almost entirely of words, it turns out to be a fairly dull interlude in the liturgy. On the other hand, if a procession brings child, parents, sponsors, utensils, and water through the congregation, possibly led by a banner and a paschal candle, a vitality may be given the event which is commensurate with its importance. A room that allows freedom is one virtue; liturgists who use the freedom are a more valuable one yet.

Musical Facilities

Provision for music in the centrum ought also to be made with a view toward flexibility of use. Pianos and portable instruments are no problem except that they require provision of current to amplifiers. The flexibility of the furnishings make their accommodation easy as far as floor space is concerned.

A number of commentators have suggested in recent years that the day of the church organ may be passed. I think one need not argue this subject; we need to recognize that it is not a requirement for good liturgies, but it is a noble instrument and useful for a great deal of music other than liturgical music. It is no more secular or religious than other instruments, and does have qualities that make it particularly useful in any place of assembly—the capacity for one musician to generate a great variety of sounds and a large volume of sound. And the number of organs being built suggests that people have not generally agreed that it is passé.

For these reasons and because organs are a mystery to most people, it seems reasonable to make some extended comments on the instrument.

From what has been said earlier about the virtues of integrity, it should be clear that the electronic church organ ought to be avoided. One can say good things about the bar room electronic; it is cheap, it is loud enough, it produces a sound which is distinctively its own. No one will mistake it for a pipe organ. But the electronic imitation of the pipe organ, which is sometimes so good an imitation that a layman can't distinguish it from the real thing, is another matter. The better the imitation the more reprehensible it is. That it is the product of ingenuity and great skill and that it is somewhat less expensive than a pipe organ make it attractive, but these attractions don't change the fact that it is a phony imitation. The alternative is, of course, the genuine pipe organ.

A pipe organ is a work of art. Its quality and value depend not only on measurable features, but on hard-to-specify but real qualities such as the builder's integrity, commitment, vision, craftsmanship and skill, sensibility, imagination, and understanding; these are reflected in his work. As with other works of art competitive bidding for pipe organ building is unreasonable.

A two-manual-and-pedal instrument of twenty-odd stops can be accepted not only as an adequate but as a really satisfying solution in almost any centrum, provided it is a good organ and is well located. The volume can be sufficient and there will be enough variety of sounds. Bigger instruments are reasonable only if the intention is to build a concert instrument. Smaller ones—as small as half a dozen stops—are providing good music in many small worship spaces. Quality is more important than size; the quality of music from a first class small instrument is likely to be better than that from a larger instrument of lower quality.

The pipes should not be in a chamber but out in the space in which the music is to be heard. Pipes may or may not be in wooden casework.

A pipe organ can be built to be movable. But even if it isn't movable it is at its best musically if it is thought of as a piece of furniture placed in a room. If an organ is considered to be a work of art, a few matters relating to production are important. The artist obviously cannot produce this work of art singlehandedly like a painter or composer or poet. He functions more like an architect. As in architecture there are areas which he controls directly and others where he depends on the skills and commitment of other people. The organ buyer should know who will be the designer of the instrument and have some idea how close his control of the execution is, and also whether the skills of those who execute the fabrication are sufficient to accomplish the goals of the designer. The voicing and finishing of an organ when it is installed is another point at which the particular sensibilities of the artist are directly applied to the instrument. And since the instrument is almost inevitably an important visual element in a room, the builder should have visual sensibilities and should deal responsively with the architect.

The quality of sound that emerges from a pipe organ depends for one thing on the characteristics of the stops or series of pipes that produce the sound. Each stop, which usually includes a pipe for each key on the keyboard (sometimes two or more for each), has its characteristic sound depending on the construction of the pipe. In any organ each stop is selected so its sound blends with that of some others and contrasts with the sound of others. Large organs obviously will have more variety and small ones less. The system of relationships of sound has a long tradition behind it, and musicians and builders are usually able to agree fairly easily about what stops ought to be included in organs of various sizes. The question of achieving in the finished instrument a proper character and relationships of the sounds is another matter; and this is the matter in which the artistry of the builder is demonstrated.

Although prescriptions cannot be made for a work of art, some comments may be useful on the state of the art. Our heritage from the nineteenth century in organ building has endowed us with some organs which attempted to imitate orchestral sounds. This was not fully possible, obviously; it has become properly archaic even as an ambition. An organ is an organ and its sounds, if it has integrity, are its own. A second heritage is a soft and distant tone that encouraged a dreamy sentimentality. This derived partly from the custom of building organs into architectural chambers and partly from the way pipes were voiced in the finishing process. This quality, which still characterizes electronic church organs almost universally, is no longer an ideal of most pipe organ builders, who wish to recover for their instrument the forthrightness,

99

clarity, and "presence" of sound that has been its long-time character.

Although all pipe organs are essentially a collection of big and small whistles controlled from keyboards, there are varieties in the systems through which the musician controls the speech of the pipes. The ancient system uses a mechanical linkage from keyboard to pipes and is called "tracker" or mechanical action. More recent systems use electrical or combined electric and pneumatic devices.

In a full mechanical action organ, both key and stop selection controls are connected mechanically with their objectives. The stop action is heavy enough and clumsy so that it is not considered practical to remove the keyboard from the pipework in full-mechanical organs. Some builders and organists set a high value on the mechanical simplicity and on the ultimate intimacy between instrument and musician which complete mechanical action provides. This arrangement, however causes a difficulty for some church musicians. It is hard for an organist to conduct a choir when he faces into the organ. The conventional solution puts the choir between console and pipe work, thus separating the two. Some organists assert that detaching the console from the pipework enables the organist to hear the sound better. This would be particularly true if the pipework extends far laterally as in large organs; but it is also true that the organist does not assume that he hears the sound exactly as an audience does any more than a violinist or a singer does. If an organ is to be movable, or the flexibility of space is a factor, the console that is tightly related to the pipework is an advantage.

Many if not most of the "trackers" or mechanical action organs built now combine mechanical action keyboards with electrical stop action. This allows the console to be separated from the pipework. The freedom is not absolute. Mechanically there may be a slight loss of responsiveness in the key touch, or it may become too heavy due to the friction and weight of the additional mechanisms involved in extending the tracker system. Some builders say that 8 to 10 feet is a practical limit for the horizontal displacement of console from pipework; but it has been demonstrated that this distance can be substantially increased by the best craftsmen. It is absolutely necessary that the pipework and console be fixed rigidly in place, and it is inadvisable to set the console in any except a rectilinear relationship to the pipe chests. It need not be centered on the pipework. And the pipework need not be symmetrical. Musically the limits of displacement are not easy to define, but the console should be as close as practicable to the pipework. A good musician values a close association to his instrument.

In an electro-pneumatic organ the connections between console and pipework are much more free because they consist of electric wiring and a small duct. The console can be movable whether the pipework is or not.

The currents of change in organ building are moving in the direction of mechanical action in preference to electro-pneumatic. This tide of change is not simply a fascination with the ancient. (Electro-pneumatic action is a 20th century innovation and has nothing to do with 19th-century Romantic music). The change is being generated by the musicians and builders who are the most sophisticated, sensitive, and committed

101

artists. The ablest organ builders are to be found in the camp of mechanical action, and it seems clear that although some of them build electro-pneumatic actions, their most intense interest is in mechanical action projects. If one wants a first rate instrument, he goes to first rate builders; nowadays they are in the tracker camp.

There are other good reasons for buying mechanical actions however. Some are practical. The durability of these instruments is better, maintenance is simpler, and the need for it less. These matters derive partly from the absence of electrical systems, and partly from the absence of the myriad of little leather pouches associated with the innumerable magnets in the electro-pneumatic systems. (Incidentally, the durability of pipe organs exceeds by far the record of electronic instruments.)

A further advantage is that the instrument is physically smaller — perhaps about half the size. The pipe spacing in an electro-pneumatic organ is governed in part by the magnets and pouches, not the pipe size; in a mechanical action organ small pipes can be set much closer together. Architecturally this is a virtue partly because a room can sometimes be smaller and thus more economical, but also because the instrument is less likely to become the magnificent overbearing display which organs often are. Musically, organs, like orchestras, are stereophonic; this is generally considered to be virtue, but it is obvious that in some circumstances it can be troublesome if the musical sources are too far separated, as they may necessarily be in a large electro-pneumatic instrument.

There are also some more important differences. It is

common that the pipework in mechanical action systems is divided physically according to the keyboard and pedal divisions and that each division is encased in a box with an open front. Such cases are acoustically somewhat similar to the resonating elements of stringed instruments — perhaps most similar to the encasements of the strings in a piano or harpsichord. The size and particularly the depth of such casework ought not be too great. Sometimes a builder will encase the pipework in an electro-pneumatic organ, but more often he will not, because the required size of the chests demands cases which are so large and deep that they don't function as effectively as those in a mechanical action organ. The subtle musical advantage offered by the casework in a tracker organ is not in practice available in an electro-pneumatic system.

A good deal of discussion has been held about the comparative responsiveness to the organist's keyboard touch between electric actions and mechanical actions. Obviously when it is an electrical magnet that controls the speech of a pipe, it will not matter whether the organist presses the key lightly, firmly, suddenly, or gradually. The magnet acts suddenly and it always acts the same. Air strikes the lip of the pipe to start the vibration and the speech of a pipe always starts the same way. If it has a chiff, it always has a chiff. In a tracker action the direct mechanical coupling between the keyboard and the valves which allow air to enter the pipes makes it possible to control the sound to a valuable degree at the initial instant when the pipe begins to speak. If the craftsmanship is refined, the wind pressure low, and the organist skillful, the organist can include or exclude the initial chiff, for instance. It should be noted that in any musical instrument the character of the initial instant of a sound is very important musically.

Some of the organists who are devoted to tracker organs however, will not place the highest value on these definable virtues. They simply say that the best music comes when the musician and his instrument are intimate, and that anything and everything that works toward this very close association is extremely important to the musical performance.

One of the side effects of mechanical action is that it makes demands on the technical capacities of the organist. Mistakes are not easily lost in a general slurry of sound. The tracker will not produce the mushy music which some people consider the hallmark of organ music but which good musicians decry. The practice of supplying a mist of music as a background for pulpit prayer, for instance, is not apt to be in the repertory of the tracker. In a time when liturgies and the character of worship are intelligently examined, when sentimentalism and soporific sweetness are recognized as religiosity rather than religion, and when directness of speech, forthrightness of manner, and objectivity are replacing the "religious mood," this is all to the good.

Mechanical action costs more than electro-pneumatic action when the standards of craftsmanship are high. Its other virtues justify this in the opinion of good organists and builders. The difference may range from 10% to 30%.

Mechanical action organs generally take longer to build. The interval from order to installation is a reflection of building time as well as of the backlog in the builders' shops. One year is a minimum in any case; a tracker may take from 18 to 36 months.

Swell boxes and tremolos may be employed in both tracker and electro-pneumatic types. The voicing of the pipes may be soft or strident in either type. The stop list and resultant sound in either type may move toward German, English, French, or Italian character; it is an illusion that trackers are necessarily German, and electro-pneumatic something else. There is some evidence that a tonal character distinctly American is being developed by some competent tracker builders. Either type may be designed as a piece of furniture; for neither is a chamber or a blower room an absolute necessity. But electro-pneumatic instruments require some space for relay boards that needs to be sound proofed. Either type of action may have 55 or 61 keys.

Choir

Except in very small groups of worshipers, a choir (or sometimes more than one) is likely to be part of the liturgy. The question of how these groups of singers ought to be related to the common body of worshipers is the subject of discussion in every building committee. And the issue is not clear, because although the choir members are, during a part of the liturgy, undistinguished from the general community, there are other episodes of the liturgy in which they provide musical leadership, and others in which they are performing artists.

It doesn't make much sense to say that the choir is different from a concert group and that therefore we should put them in a choir loft where they aren't seen and are not heard to the best advantage. If

the choir sometimes sings music that requires rehear-
sals, high skills, and the other attitudes and facilities
of a concert group, and sings it for people who listen
like a concert audience, the distinction between the
concert and the worship situation is illusory.

Sometimes it is said that the choir is singing for God
and the implication is that it doesn't much matter
whether they are properly heard by people. This is
sophistry. The choir should ideally be located where
its voices can be heard well. This means that ideally
they should sing toward the people, not to their backs.
And the practice currently popular in new Roman
Catholic buildings where they are in front pews with
the listeners behind them is not reasonable. Any solution has its limitations, and particular circumstances
may lead to varied solutions. The possibility of the
choir leaving its seats for the special parts of the liturgy
when they act like performers should not be ignored.

But the choir's main duty is to sing *with* the congregation as its leaders in song, and their normal, if not
continuous location, should support this intention. For
this kind of function they may need no risers; for
other music they very likely will. Such risers may well
be built from components identical or similar to those
provided for the principal platform. If organist and
choir director are one person, a different and more
difficult arrangement is required from the circumstances where two musicians are involved. In addition
a director may need a podium and a music stand.

Processions

Movement and spectacle is characteristic of celebrations; it is proper that such things as processions
should be part of Christian celebrations, as they indeed

106

have been. It is not difficult to provide for movement of various kinds in a centrum where flexibility is the rule. Indeed, one may need to expect it if the flexibility is properly exploited. Even if a conventional sacristy is provided (which is not really necessary since the sacristy is no longer a place of liturgical prayer), its proximity to the platform cannot be assured. If a choir is robed there needs to be some place for robing, and the path from robing room to choir seating implies some sort of procession. But other kinds of processions related to the eucharistic ritual, the baptismal ritual, and other occasional rituals can be planned and accommodated. In any case the custom of providing the clergy a special doorway where they can enter as if from the wings onto the stage doesn't make much sense. And we surely ought to free ourselves from the notion that an entrance procession has to start as far from the altar as possible and end as close to it as possible.

Processions are generally led and sometimes concluded by standard bearers. In the processions of the church the principal standard has usually been the processional cross. The logic of stationing this standard finally at some point far distant from the people holds only in the traditional processional plan church, of course. In a centrum, logic suggests that it stand not as remote as possible, but perhaps right among the people. Such a cross, if it is to be carried, cannot be very large, but even a small cross is large enough. One doesn't need to suppose that there must be a gigantic symbol somewhere, as if making a cross big demonstrates superior piety.

I have been proposing also for some time that we replace the Latin cross by using the Greek. These are

Two processional crosses; the one at the right contains the Greek cross.

the reasons: The Greek cross is the more ancient symbolic form. The processes by which it came to be used are not entirely clear; but its origin is most likely the Greek letter Chi — the initial of Christ — turned 45 degrees. It may have suggested the Good Friday cross to the early Christians, but this is unlikely since the actual instrument of execution was more like a T. The Greek cross most likely attracted the early Christians because it is graphically a simple strong thing, because its form carries the suggestion of universality, and because it has some hint of explosive joy appropriate to the Easter hope, which occupied their minds as the denouement of the Good Friday tragedy.

Although the Latin cross appeared in some pictorial representations, its use seems to have been uncommon until Anselm, at the end of the first millenium, focused the theological consciousness of the Western church on Good Friday with his soteriology. Thereafter it became the rule to place a crucifix on altars.

The iconoclastic reformers removed the corpus and left the Protestants with a symbol which is the image of an instrument of torture. We have become used to this curiosity so that we most often forget what it is, or suppose that the absence of a corpus is an adequate symbol for resurrection. Would an empty electric chair symbolize resurrection? Or would we accept the electric chair as a proper symbol of the Christian faith if Jesus had been executed in this century?

There is something ironic furthermore about what we do with the Latin cross by decorating it, sweetening its shapes and otherwise turning it into a thing which is no longer a good symbol of Good Friday.

The Greek cross then ought to be the principal symbol. But we should certainly not forget Good Friday; and at proper times and seasons, like Lent, some form of the Latin cross, unsweetened, and with the corpus, ought to replace it. Or perhaps the tragic image ought to supplement the joyful one. For there is no reason to avoid the image altogether.

Lighting

Other symbolic accoutrements customary in worship spaces continue to be appropriate. Candles are used in our domestic and other celebrations, and have the same values when they are used during worship. They are a universal symbol; we respond to their warmth, their light, liveliness; the immateriality and potential power of flame suggest spirituality. There is reason to distribute them in the room, rather than to use them only at the Lord's table. The paschal candle with its relationship to baptism and to the funeral ceremonies deserves more general usage. The tradition of having two communion candles on the eucharistic table is, I should think, more dubious. The symbolic association of these lights with the two natures of Christ is purely a literary notion; nothing about the symbol suggests the meaning it is supposed to carry. We could well afford to abandon that convention.

Another convention that gives a false impression is the sanctuary light or eternal light. Anyone, I suppose, would recognize the impropriety of such a device in a centrum. What the centrum intends to demonstrate is that God is not attached to particular places. The sanctuary light implies just the opposite. Roman Catholic piety associates this symbol with the presence of the reserved host, and current ideals in Roman Catholic practice direct that tabernacle and light should be in a separate room.

Paraments

Any altar-guild approach that supposes there is a "proper" way to do things and seeks simply to follow the "rules," should be abandoned. The best taste, skill, and imagination we use in our domestic environments is needed in the worship space. There are no rules that take precedence over this.

The use of colored paraments related to the seasons of the liturgical year is a venerable practice and a logical one. In our homes we often cover the dining table with a decorative cloth between meals and lay a white table cloth over it at meal time. This domestic practice is the model of liturgical usage. We shouldn't suppose that the fabrics we use at worship need to be brocades when we wouldn't dream of using brocade at home. And we shouldn't suppose that we need to have a matched set all in similar fabrics and shapes or that the number and colors need to be limited to the conventional four or five, or that Advent and Lent have to be the same, or that the fabric shouldn't be varied through the long Pentecost season, or that fabrics have to have an ecclesiastical symbol embroidered on them and gold fringes. Few of us would care to have any fringes at all in our fabrics at home.

It has been customary in liturgical settings to match the altar cloth with a pulpit antependium and perhaps with a similar fabric for the lectern. The practice of draping a speaker's stand may derive from times when books were precious and were carried to the podium wrapped in cloth. This is no longer the circumstance, and we shouldn't feel hesitant about omitting the antependium altogether.

Among the fabrics that might be brought into the centrum one deserves special comment, the national flag. There are times when its presence in the centrum is clearly appropriate, such as when a political meeting is held. But however much we love our country and honor those who have rallied around the banner over two centuries, the liturgical event is not the appropriate place to make a display of patriotic loyalty. In a country where church and state are separate, it makes no more sense to have the flag in a church than to have the cross in the court room. Indeed, the implication that the church exists under the aegis of the nation is false as is the reverse. And the custom of pairing the papal or the so-called Christian flag with the national ensign on a pair of twin standards implies a parallel which just doesn't exist.

There are many ways to give expression to our patriotism most of which have more reality about them than simply exhibiting a flag, and I have no quarrel with the patriot. But when we worship we must set our minds on the Kingdom of God and on our membership in a human community that extends far beyond nationality and geography. Those who assert the propriety of the national flag in the liturgical assembly usually say that it is a reminder to pray for the nation and of the duties of citizenship. This doesn't explain why they want the paired flags, of course, nor why they think the flags should have a dominant location, nor why there shouldn't be state, county and city flags, or the emblems of any other institution for which we ought to pray and for which we bear responsibility.

Flowers

Flowers and plants should be used with freedom, not simply to emphasize the importance of the table, but to make the whole room a place of celebration. It may be that the best place for a bouquet is not the table, but at the entrance or in the foyer where people can appreciate not only color but fragrance. Green plants are as good in a centrum as in other pleasant places; obviously it is improper to use artificial plants.

Ecclesiastical Images

The idea that the architecture of a centrum should not be adorned with ecclesiastical images does not mean we must be iconoclasts. There ought to be in any good environment the association of building, sculpture, and painting that occurs in many historical periods.

Many people are troubled that the close cooperation among several kinds of the visual artists to make a complete setting is not often attempted anymore, and that where it is attempted, the results are often unsuccessful. Indeed in the present state of the arts the most successful relationships are present where the building is conceived separately from painting and sculpture. This relationship enhances both the spatial setting and the works of art which it shelters.

A centrum, then, may be an unadorned structure. But a good space will be hospitable not only to people but to art and artifacts, and they can be used freely. There are however, two caveats. One is that the work of art associated with worship ought to be a good work of art. The temptation for a congregation to accept and use any painting, reproduction, or trinket that is offered in good faith by a member is a strong one, and every congregation ought to devise a screening and purchase system where important events are not trivialized by the presence of paltry art and artifacts. One means of doing this is to establish some knowledgeable and responsible and courageous person as arbiter of these decisions. Such a rule might keep some careless and ugly banners out of sight, for one thing. And it would almost inevitably avoid some of the trash that passes for religious painting. It needs to be said that if the quality of architecture is affective, so is the quality of art and artifact. They also need to be the work of good artists.

The second caveat concerns not quality but quantity. We need not have many things, all displayed at once. Better to have one very good thing than a dozen mediocre things. And if you have two very good things they need not be displayed together. Worship ought to be focused; and works of art are means to this end; they are not decorative space-fillers.

Stained Glass

To conclude this chapter I want to comment on the use of stained glass, not as an opportunity for the introduction of ecclesiastical images as has been its traditional use in church buildings, but for its practical virtues. In any place of assembly light control is a problem with which a designer must deal. Glare and external distractions must be avoided, and still sufficient light must be allowed to enter. Colored glass provides one of several means of accomplishing this. If leaded glass is used, the cames provide a filligree which also adds to the intimate character of a space. Most stained glass designers like to think of their work in terms of images, and even when they work in non-objective designs they tend to envision a window as a work of art which ought to call attention to itself. But if the designer can be induced to see the glazed opening as simply a light filter with colors that are lovely and patterns that are elegant, stained glass can be a good way to deal with light. It is a material that has virtues in any structure, and although its recent uses and its most spectacular uses have been mainly in ecclesiastical buildings, there is nothing inherently "religious" in stained glass, and its use in non-cultic architecture is increasing.

5

The Renewal
of Church Buildings

Is it really possible that the congregations of America
are going to give up their ecclesiastical prejudices?
Can they possibly be persuaded to believe that sixteen
hundred years of church building tradition have been
in error, even if they concede that the three hundred
years previously were right? Isn't it inevitable that
American church people will try to settle on compromise if they are swayed away from ecclesiasticism
at all? And won't that compromise result in a lot of
lukewarm nothingness?

But worst of all, suppose here and there a building
committee decides not to build a "church," but something else, perhaps a centrum? Is it going to make any
consequential difference at all for the church generally,
so long as several hundred thousand ecclesiastical
monuments stand about the country teaching our
children things that Jesus never taught? If the character of the church's buildings is as significant as architects think it is, isn't it true that something has to be

done about or to or with the existing buildings to quench their false witness and make them servants of a servant church?

One can look with some cheer on what has happened in worship among the Roman Catholics over a period of a decade; radical changes are not really impossible. On the other hand not much has changed in Protestant church buildings during the same decade. And it is true that among the Catholics too, although altars have been brought forward as tables, communion rails abandoned, baptismal rites brought out of seclusion, choir screens removed, and other changes made, these things have not been done because the conception of the place has changed. The church building is still thought to be an ecclesiastical enclave, almost without exception.

But suppose that a congregation does want to make the real change away from the House of God to the house of the people. A number of severe problems inhibit the freedom, and they are worth discussing because this is just what every congregation ought to be doing and a few have already done. Compromises are inevitable and often painful. And the wisdom to make the fruitful compromise in these circumstances requires the broadest understanding, the finest sensitivity both liturgical and architectural, and the best skills available. No one should imagine that because a building is old and the project is only a remodelling, it can be put in the hands of a properties committee or a mediocre professional.

The major impediment to ideal accomplishment is likely to be the existing structure — a sound structure enclosing a space that is both wrong and intractable.

It is encouraging to know that the sixteenth-century reformers, confronting the equally intractable buildings they inherited from their medieval ancestors, were sometimes courageous and did not hesitate to make drastic changes. Sometimes they closed off the ancient choirs entirely and used them for smaller assemblies or for teaching places. Sometimes they set the seating so that it faced the pulpit half-way down the nave (which was possible with flat floors). These same possibilities are open to some parishes today.

But under some circumstances no such transformation is possible. There are buildings that would become chaotic and ugly rooms if such radical changes were made. And there are a few church buildings of such architectural excellence that they must be respected and changes made with great caution. In almost any congregation there are people who think that theirs is one of these architectural treasures and resist change because of it. Let it be said that this is in fact rarely true; there are not really many buildings so fine that a good designer can't improve them in the process of change, or at least maintain the original level of architectural quality. And there are many that are bad in so many ways that almost any reasonable change is an improvement.

The same comment can be made about the decorations, the art and the artifacts, that contribute so heavily to the burden of ecclesiasticism in existing buildings. Occasionally there are stained glass windows of superb beauty. But much more often the stained glass is imitative and trivial, and people admire it because they have paid what they have thought to be a high price for it or have learned to love it because it is so familiar. There is sometimes sculpture or painting or

117

carving or other sorts of artifacts of real quality. But much more often these things also are derivative and inconsequential.

If a parish has questions about the virtue of their property, they can sometimes get a useful opinion from a museum curator. If he thinks a thing to be so good that he would like to have it in his museum, perhaps then it ought to be kept — or perhaps it ought to be given to the museum.

The criteria that ought to govern the erection of a new structure for a church ought to guide the renewal of existing buildings. And though we cannot expect the results to conform in many respects to what we might wish, there are projects that have been accomplished that demonstrate how fruitful a vigorous and thoughtful effort can be.

Examples of Renewal

St. Katherine's is a parish church on the east edge of Baltimore where a change in the neighborhood has made it interracial and otherwise mixed. The building is a massive, pseudo-Romanesque bastion of the sort where most people would suppose change to be absolutely unmanageable. Here Fr. Joseph Connolly, a priest whose sense that liturgy and human concern belong together, is leading the parish to immerse themselves in providing for the welfare of all the people in the area. He now calls his church building a "community service center." The vast and formerly empty nave has been cleared of pews and other hindrances to fuller use. It has become the meeting place for any kind of assembly that needs a place, and movable screens can separate different kinds of activities that occur simultaneously. Children of all colors swarm. Rock music, dances, clinics, educational enterprises, eating and drinking, even a homosexual group have been given shelter. For if Jesus didn't reject the company of publicans and prostitutes, why should the church be less hospitable? Architecturally the project is far from ideal; the budget for change has been trifling. And much more could and will be done. But the building has become the tool of a program of service, which is the proper starting point.

When the monks at Gethsemani Abbey in Trappist, Kentucky, decided to renew the Abbey church, it was a century-old stone structure with a lofty and elaborately decorated plaster-vaulted interior. In a hope not only to improve the liturgical arrangements but to get rid of the artificiality of the surroundings, they stripped away the contrived gothic lining. What they exposed was a noble space as elegant as it is simple. Courageously and doubtless painfully, they cleared out what was really stage-scenery, and saved what was really good of the ancient structure. Into this clean and ingenuous room they moved some well-designed new chairs and the necessary new liturgical furnishings. The result is a sparse but beautiful room that is a better image by far of the orderly and self-denying character of their religious commitment. The unadorned surfaces provide a setting where people are seen as important, and despite the great size of the space, the texture and scale of surfaces and furnishings make it hospitable and full of hope.

Christ Church Cathedral, the center of the Episcopal diocese of St. Louis, is a neo-Gothic structure built over a hundred years ago to the designs of Richard Upjohn, who was one of the best architects of his

(Above) Gethsemani Abbey Church before renovation. (Below) the renovation reveals a simple and excellent structure.

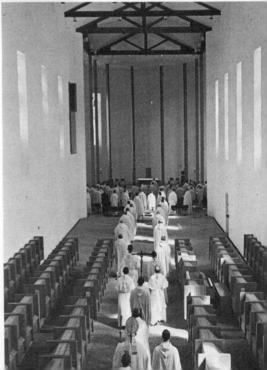

time. It is a paragon of the Ecclesiological Movement. But the 1950s and '60s found it most often near-empty when it had once been full, and entirely empty most of the time, serving only the needs of a diminishing parish, and becoming more a burden than a joy. The dean of Christ Church recognized that downtown St. Louis could be a healthier place if the church would help. So a careful and serious enterprise was begun. The pews were taken out and replaced by chairs. The chancel was fitted with a scrim curtain so the nave and transepts can be understood as the total space. A metal gallery was designed with sympathetic taste and installed at the triforium level to serve as a source for special lighting. A modular and movable platform was introduced, and portable liturgical furniture constructed. Now Christ Church is not only a better place for the liturgy, but it is used for many events that attract and engage people of all sorts. The platform is sometimes moved to the center of the nave for theater in the round. Sometimes it is moved to the narthex end and the seating reversed for concerts. So a moribund parish has become viable again because its horizons of service have been extended, and a fine work of architecture has become much less a "house of God" and much more a meeting place for all of his children.

A fire damaged the chapel of Texas Lutheran College in Seguin, Texas, but failed to destroy the structure. It was agreed that the repair should not only restore but renew so that the building could not only serve the liturgical life better but other "secular" events of campus life. Designed in the pattern of the ecclesiological tradition with cruciform plan and a gloomy atmosphere, the building was typical of hundreds of church buildings of the 1940s and '50s. Reconstruction involved replacing pews with chairs, the installation of

121

The renovation of Christ Church Cathedral made it a fruitful servant of many good purposes.

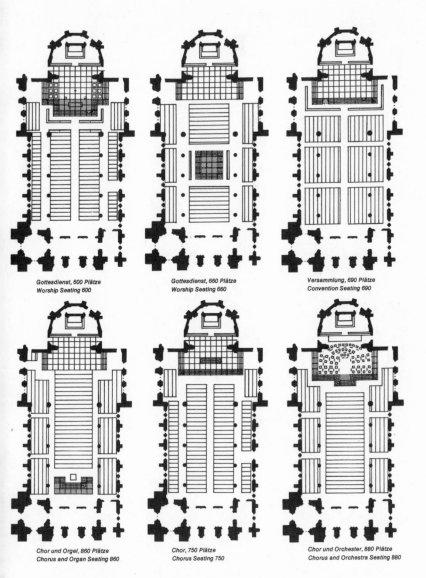

Gottesdienst, 600 Plätze
Worship Seating 600

Gottesdienst, 660 Plätze
Worship Seating 660

Versammlung, 690 Plätze
Convention Seating 690

Chor und Orgel, 860 Plätze
Chorus and Organ Seating 860

Chor, 750 Plätze
Chorus Seating 750

Chor und Orchester, 880 Plätze
Chorus and Orchestra Seating 880

Movable seating and platform units can be used in a variety of configurations.

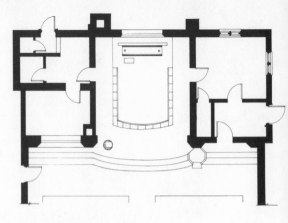

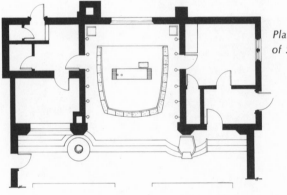

Plans for the staged remodeling of St. John's Lutheran Church

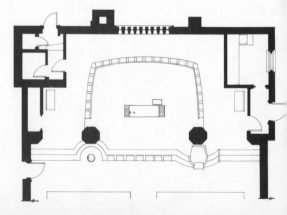

124

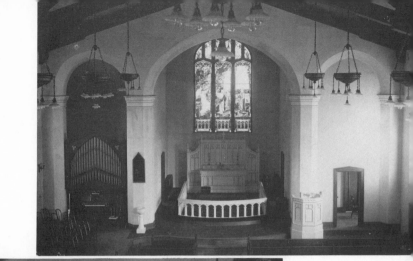

The existing structure provided limiting factors; changes improved the liturgical use and architectural character.

a movable screen to close off the existing chancel (which can now be a stage, a platform, or a meeting room), a platform of modular units that can be changed as occasion demands, and movable liturgical furnishings. In addition a quarry-tile floor replaced the existing asphalt tile, a change that gave the room a new dignity; the plaster walls and timber roof structure were painted in vigorous color. Mechanical and electrical systems were improved to make the building comfortable under all conditions. So the disaster of fire was made into an occasion of profit for the general life of the institution.

We should not depend on catastrophe to give impetus to renewal, of course; nor need the process be a swift and comprehensive one. It may be possible to accomplish more by entering a phased sequence of change. This is the route taken by St. John's Church in Northfield, Minnesota. In this fifty-year-old church a process began with the installation of a new mechanical-action organ in a rear choir loft, thus voiding the chamber next to the deep chancel where the earlier instrument had been. A second stage opened up this space and the corresponding room across the chancel so that the continuity between nave and chancel is much improved. A table replaced the remote altar, and though a communion kneeler still remains, it now arches around beyond the table so congregation and communicants face each other. A stained glass version of an oil painting that formerly confronted the worshippers was removed despite the qualms of parishioners who had learned to love it. The opening was enlarged and glazed simply with brilliant red. The result has been received happily; the color itself conveys a sense of joy, love, hope, and vitality that is more convincing than the pictorial image ever was.

Unhappily a sloping floor made any reorientation or the use of chairs too expensive. Further changes both utilitarian and otherwise are anticipated.

Whatever the limitations may be in existing structures, and however short of the ideal the final result of reconstruction or renewal may be, there is a force in this sort of accomplishment that gives it value. In new structures we expect a difference; it is taken for granted. But when a consequential change is made in an old structure — and this applies even more if the structure is not a decrepit or ancient one — people look for the reasons for change. And if they find the reasons good, the goal has been achieved. It isn't buildings that need change but the people, and the renewal of buildings is only a means to help people understand the church and their faith as it ought to be understood.

LIST OF ILLUSTRATIONS